H. S. K_____
1952

Old Furniture & Woodwork

METALWORK

A STORY OUTLINE

By DONALD SMITH

This companion volume to *Old Furniture and Woodwork* deals from the points of view of the craft-worker with the development of metalwork from the earliest prehistoric times. There are chapters on The Blacksmith, The Sword-smith and Armourer, The Goldsmith and Silversmith, The Dinner Table, Lighting and Heating, etc. The book is very fully illustrated, both from drawings specially made by the author, and by about 50 photographs showing examples of metalwork of every period and type from the Bronze Age to the present day.

Demy 8vo.

Published by
B. T. BATSFORD LTD.

CABINET ON STAND, with Marquetry Inlay of Flowers and Birds, *circa* 1700.

OLD FURNITURE & WOODWORK

An Introductory Historical Survey

By

DONALD SMITH, F.R.G.S., F.R.Hist.S.

*Author of " English Windmills," and " Pigeon
Cotes and Dove Houses of Essex "*

*Illustrated from
Photographs and Drawings*

B. T. BATSFORD LTD.

LONDON ★ NEW YORK

TORONTO   SYDNEY

TO MY MOTHER

First Edition . 1937
Second Edition . 1947
Third Edition . 1949

Made and printed in Great Britain by The Aberdeen University Press, Ltd., for the Publishers, B. T. BATSFORD, Ltd. LONDON : 15 North Audley Street, W. 1 and Malvern Wells, Worcestershire. NEW YORK : 122 East 55th Street. TORONTO : 480–6 University Avenue. SYDNEY : 156 Castlereagh Street.

INTRODUCTION

ALL people have ancestors. Some families can trace their descent for many generations. In the same way the chair upon which we sit, the table at which we have our meals, all furniture in fact, has its ancestors and, in most cases, an extremely interesting family history. One piece of furniture may be related to another, perhaps recently or perhaps in the distant past, some, after the lapse of many years take again some feature that had not appeared in the family for many, many years. Some articles of furniture have risen in the world and are found, decorated with the utmost skill, in State Rooms or are preserved with every care in Museums built specially to contain them ; others have descended to lowly uses and are found only in kitchens, workshops or cow-sheds. Just as the fashions of our clothes and the design of our houses never remain constant for long, but change steadily with the changing years, so the fashions of furniture change likewise, adapting themselves unceasingly to the changing ways of living of the people who use the furniture.

This book tries to tell very briefly the life-story of some of the most important kinds of furniture that have kept man company for many ages. The illustrations and the text go together ; the illustrations are perhaps the more important. More important still, is the study of the furniture itself. Start with the kitchen at home, and, having read this book, go from room to room, and see if some of the tables and cupboards and chairs have not a story to tell you. If they do, then the purpose of the book, has, in some way, met with success.

* * * * * * * * * *

The book may be compared to an atlas. We speak of " reading a map ". It is only the skilled person who can really " read " a map and get all the information that it offers. It is part of the purpose of this book to help the student to read the pictures aright, and then to seek out those things the pictures represent and to study them also. History books tell of men's doings, of their actions and thoughts. It is only very recently that they have begun to tell also of what men have made. And yet, if we regard the lives of the great number of ordinary people around us, we shall see that by far the most important things about their lives is not their thoughts or their relations with other people, but the fact that they are engaged in making, or in helping to make, something or other. If we could have a complete series of things that have been made since man first began to make until the present time, we should be able, with a near approach to the exact truth, to read the story of mankind.

This book intends to take one substance (medium) that men of all ages have used, and to try to show what things have been fashioned from it. The substances from which man has made things for his everyday use have been surprisingly few, and of these few it is perhaps possible to say that wood has been the most important. Men have existed without metals, they have lived almost entirely without the use of stone, but always and in almost every part of the habitable globe, wood has stood ready for the hand of man, for his utensils, for his building, for his transport. It has been so always. The first boat and the first aeroplane were made of wood. The first movable type for printing was of wood blocks, and to-day the large letters for poster-printing are cut from wood. So soon as man moved out from cave homes he erected shelters of branches, and when the Norwegian people of to-day wished to honour their king they built him a forest home, *Kongssäter*, entirely of timber. Man has worshipped wooden idols and his children have played with wooden toys. Furniture of all times has been of wood. It is from wood that musical instruments have been made, and the same material supplies the bats and rackets, the cues and clubs for our games. Weapons and agricultural implements, looms and spinning wheels, skis and sabots, pipes and knitting needles, " hearts of oak " and 'varsity " eights," these and an innumerable host of other objects and articles of daily use have been made from the same material.

It is the purpose of this book that its illustrations should lead outwards to an interest in that great number of serviceable things of wood that have accompanied man's life-story, and should help those who see, to read what each thing has to tell.

D. S.

September, 1937.

CONTENTS

ACKNOWLEDGMENT

WHILE the majority of the illustrations are from specially made drawings by the author or from photographs in the publishers' collection, the publishers would like to acknowledge their indebtedness to the following : The British Museum, for Plate I (7) ; the late Brian C. Clayton, for Plate VII (1) ; Mr. Herbert Cescinsky, for the frontispiece and Plate XVI (1) ; the late Richard Glazier, for Plate VII (2), which appears in his *Manual of Historic Ornament ;* Mr. Herbert Felton, for Plate VIII (1) ; The Metropolitan Museum of Art, New York, for Plate XVI (2) ; The Norwegian State Railways, for Plate II (1) ; and the Victoria and Albert Museum, for Plates II (2), VIII (2), IX (2), XI (2), XIV (2), XIV (1), XVII (2), XXVI (2), and XXXIII (4).

NOTE.—*Be sure you read the Notes on the Plates at the end of the book, when you have read each chapter*

CHAPTER I

ANCIENT WOODCRAFT

WHEN speaking of something that is very old indeed we usually say that it is as old as the hills, but when speaking of things made by man, it would be truer to say " as old as the rivers," for it was in the river valleys that *workmen* really became *craftsmen*. An incredible time ago, in the valley of the Nile, men became skilful in the use of tools.

The Egyptians believed that they would actually live again with their earthly bodies and that they could take with them things that would be useful in the after-life. They believed that, beside actual things, representations of things, whether painted or drawn or made in miniature, could be endued with spiritual life in the spirit world and serve the needs of the dead owner. It was even believed that figures of the dead person, carved in wood or stone, or painted upon a wall, could perform any laborious or unpleasant task or duty for the person after death. Because of all this, very great care was bestowed upon the placing and building of the burial places so that they *should not be disturbed*.

Because the climate was so dry, and because the good land was so limited that the burial sites were placed on the edge of the desert where there was either a waste of sand, or a rocky escarpment in which tombs could be hewn, and because the tomb entrances were so carefully hidden, it is still possible to find tombs with their contents undisturbed after all these thousands of years, and we have (1) a wonderful selection of the work of craftsmen who laboured from at least five thousand years before Christ, and (2) on the walls of the tomb chambers and on written papyri an unrivalled pictorial record of the life and work of untold generations of Egyptian people.

These records and actual remains make clear the extraordinary fact that the Egyptian woodworker was making chairs and tables before even the Celts (Ancient Britons) came to these islands. Furniture was made in Egypt several thousand years before the Romans came to Britain, which was being copied in England when the Battle of Waterloo was fought. There is a box (a coffin) (i. 1) in the British Museum which is certainly 5000 and possibly 7000 years old. The back and front are *framed*, that is, the " rails " (the cross pieces at top and bottom) are tenoned into the " stiles " (the upright pieces at the ends). The thick boards forming the panels are pierced from side to side and long slats or keys are driven through.

I

The panels fit into "rebates" (grooves cut in the edge) of the rails, and the whole box is fastened with wooden pegs. The miracle is that such framing was not done by English carpenters until the reign of Henry IV. Many Egyptian mummy cases and the huge cases (called sarcophagi) which contained them were of wood. The huge wooden slabs were squared and finished exquisitely. The corners were "mitred," they were pegged and had a "key" at top and bottom (i. 2, 3). The lids were at first flat slabs, but later were "coved" (rounded like a trunk lid), and finally, when the coffin was shaped to the figure within, the lid was carded to represent its occupant.

Boxes with hinged or with sliding lids, boxes to hold vases, boxes to hold figures of carven wood, or stone or clay which were to labour for the deceased in the next world, toilet boxes, caskets, framed chests to be slung on poles and carried on the shoulders of slaves, were made thousands of years before dug-out chests were made in England.

The same story can be told of chairs and stools. The earliest remains show separate legs, carved in the shape of ox or goat or lions' legs *tenoned* into the frame of the seat. From the earliest times chairs were made with a grace of outline, a strength of construction and an obvious comfort in use that has never been surpassed. Footstools and stools for workmen were made in abundance and in great variety. One stool in particular with folding legs and a web seat (like our camp stools) is probably the ancestor of the folding and legged chairs that have been made ever since.

Side by side with chairs and stools the tables were equally advanced in construction. Tables and benches, with legs, sometimes shaped, sometimes plain, sometimes joined with "stretchers," sometimes standing independently, are equally common. Most common seems to have been a table with a single pedestal leg, the like of which was not made in England until mahogany was used not two hundred years ago.

Several facts stand out clearly as we study the woodwork of the Egyptian craftsman. The first is that he made extraordinary progress at first, and then appears to have stood still for centuries. Probably his furniture, etc., suited its purpose so well that there was no need to experiment. Secondly, for decoration he relied mainly upon colour. The wood was a base which was painted, or covered with a plaster composition which was gilded or painted, or it was sheathed with precious metals or with a mosaic of precious stones, glass or porcelain. In one form of woodcraft the Egyptian did advance continuously until he attained a wonderfully perfected skill, and that was in carving human beings and animals "in the round."

Travelling to the north we come to Greece. Here there were no such tombs as in Egypt, there were different beliefs with regard to the dead, and centuries of warfare destroyed all but the merest trifles of old Greek woodwork. The British Museum has a little box that shows that the Greeks knew and used the corner locking joint—

PLATE I

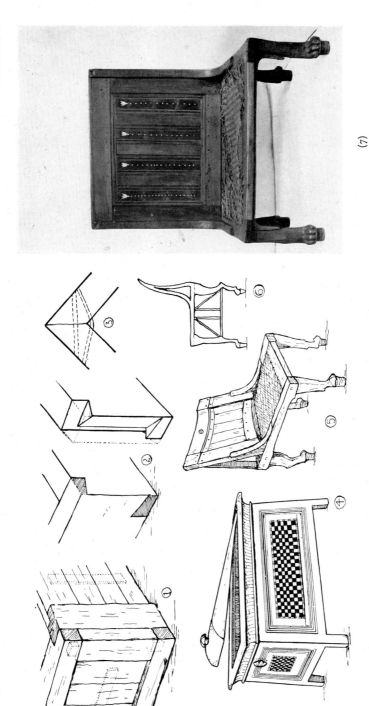

(7)

EGYPTIAN WOODCRAFT.—1. Corner of a Coffin.   2 and 3. Joints.   4. Inlaid and Painted Casket.   5 and 6. Chairs.   7. Inlaid Chair.

PLATE II

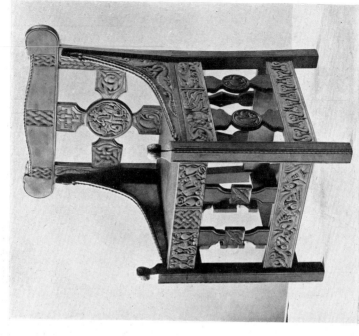

(2)

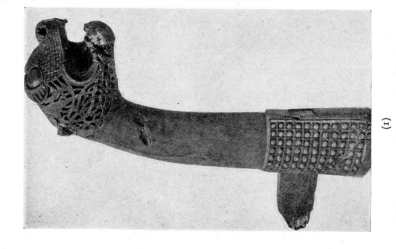

(1)

SCANDINAVIAN ORNAMENT, Ninth and Tenth Centuries.—1. Carved Bed-post from the Oseberg Ship.　2. Early Norwegian Chair (copy of the original).

the sort of joint used in machine-made soap boxes. We are not so interested in Greek furniture, however, as in Greek ornament. The Greek artists perfected certain forms of ornament to such a degree, and they were seen to be so lovely and exquisitely suited to their purpose, that they were repeated endlessly. Chief among them were the " fret," which in the very beginning was probably a rope pattern ; the use of the acanthus leaf, and of various mouldings of which the " egg and dart " is the best known. The Greeks also perfected different ways of decorating the capitals of columns and the various methods of grooving or " fluting " the surface of columns.

All these " tricks of the trade " were borrowed by the Romans, who mixed them with ideas from other peoples they conquered. All these borrowings made Roman art very florid and varied. It became more naturalistic. Whole masses of fruit and flowers were carved as festoons and " swags." Strange beasts, birds, and the human figure were introduced. All of this was joined with a very free use of the round-headed arch.

This may seem to be a long way from the woodwork of furniture-making, but really it is most important. Three times at least in English history decoration in this country has been most deeply influenced by the art of the Greek and Roman, (1) after the Normans came, (2) during the Renaissance, in the reigns of Henry VIII and Elizabeth, and (3) from about 1750 till 1800, when the greatest of English furniture makers, Thomas Chippendale, was working to the designs of an architect called Robert Adam. History tells us, and we can read in the shapes of chairs and tables, in the carven decoration of chests and picture frames, of cupboards and staircases, in the inlaid panels of bed-heads and bureaux, and in a thousand other instances the immense influence that Greek and Roman design has had upon the woodworker's craft in England.

Ancient Woodcraft of the North

England has been a meeting-place of men and ideas. The south has sent us influences, ways of building and of decorating, but it has been from the north that her people have come. They came from the shores of the North Sea, from the Baltic, from Norway and Sweden, from Denmark and North Germany, from the Low Countries around the Rhine mouth. It was these folk who felled the trees and shaped the logs, who built house and home.

It was the dark and cold of the northern winter that brought the " hall " into being, the large room built around a central hearth which gave heat and light to all, to free-born and serf, to master and man, where all could meet and work, could feast or take counsel, could sleep or play. In some cases the same roof even covered the stables and byres. The Lord had a " high seat " from which he could see all that took place. A bench ran around the walls. Forms and stools, with trestle tables, were the furniture.

There was the same need in England of gathering around the

PLATE III

GREEK AND ROMAN DECORATION.—1. Various Mouldings.   2. Various Beadings.
3. Palmate Bands.   4. Torus Mouldings.   5. The Interlace and Guilloche.
6. Modillions; Nulling and Acanthus Mouldings.   7. Doric, Ionic and Corinthian Capitals. ; Roman Arch and Rosette.   8. Greek Frets.

hearth for warmth and light, and for many centuries our forefathers continued to build and to furnish as their forefathers had built and furnished in their home-lands beyond the sea.

In just the same way as in Egypt we have gleaned much of what we know of the craft-work of the north from the burial places of people of high rank. In Scandinavia the most famous of these are the ship burial sites on the shorelands of Oslo Fiord. In these the ship and personal belongings of the owner were buried within a huge mound. These are not so old as the Egyptian tombs, but the contents show the wonderful skill that the northern woodworker had attained, both in construction and in certain forms of decorative carving. We must remember, too, that the skilled craftsmen was honoured in the north, and we read that among the accomplishments of King Olaf, the Saint of Norway, he was " very handy, and very exact and knowing in all kinds of smith-work, whether he himself or others made the thing."

The story of English woodcraft is very largely the story of generations of native workmen, whose ancestors came from the northern lands, adapting themselves time and again to new ideas and new timbers that have come to these shores from the south.

THINGS TO DO

1. If there is a Museum or a good Library handy, go and see if it contains any Egyptian woodwork, or books containing pictures of Egyptian craftsmen at work, or copies of papyrus or wall paintings with representations of furniture.
2. Copy as much as you can for your notebook collections.
3. In the workshop make copies of Egyptian wood-jointing. Full-size copies of Ushabti boxes and cases for Canopic jars can be made, and models of much of the furniture.
4. Draw all you can of Greek ornament.
5. Model in chalk or plasticine the capitals of the Greek orders.
6. Study attentively any representation of Greek or Roman ornament or architecture.
7. Never pass a technical word if you are not perfectly sure of its meaning. Underline them when they first occur if the book is your own. Keep a notebook and enter the *word*, its *derivation*—this is often very interesting—and its *meaning* or meanings, and add *sketches*.

    What is meant by : escarpment, papyri, rail, stile, rebates, sarcophagus, mitre, coved, tenon, stretcher, fret, moulding, fluting, swag, trestle ?
8. Make a model of a Northern Hall (see Airne's " Story of Saxon and Norman Britain ").

CHAPTER II

THE CHEST

FURNITURE is made to serve three chief purposes, (1) to put things on, (2) to put things in, (3) to sit or lie on. The simplest forms serving these three purposes are (1) the shelf, (2) the box, and (3) the stool.

There are odds and ends, such as screens, which may be called miscellanea.

The number of names given to boxes and box-like articles of furniture are some indication to the importance of the box. In France the words mainly used were " coffre " (Eng. coffer) and " huche " (Eng. hutch). So important was the making of chests that " huchier " became the name of all furniture-makers, and in England the cofferer gave way to the cabinet-maker who made chests full of little drawers and whose name was adopted by the most skilled of woodworkers. In England the word " chest " was usually used for a large lidded box, as in " parish chest," church chest, linen chest, dower chest, tool chest, tea chest, chest of drawers, medicine chest, etc. " Case " is not so common, although show-case, clock-case, book-case, case of instruments, suit-case and attaché-case are well known. Boxes we have innumerable, as well as the special use of the word as in knife-box (which usually is not a box), match-box (which usually is a little drawer), snuff-boxes, work-boxes, alms-box and poor-box, and not least the Christmas box, which was a collecting box in which small coins were put to give children, apprentices, servants, lather-boys, etc., a Christmas treat, etc. The small box is a casket, or, it may be, a caddy. In churches there are " shrines " which are chests for containing precious relics, and in the church-yard there are coffins.

The chest is stated to be undoubtedly the oldest form of furniture. We have spoken already of Egyptian chests and boxes. There is no doubt that many of the Israelities worked as skilled craftsmen in Egypt, and that Bezaleel was one of these. We read of him :

" And I have filled him with the spirit of God, in wisdom and in understanding, and in knowledge, and in all manner of workmanship. To devise cunning works, to work in gold, and in silver, and in brass, and in cutting of stones, to set them, *and in carving of timber*, and in all manner of workmanship."

6

PLATE IV

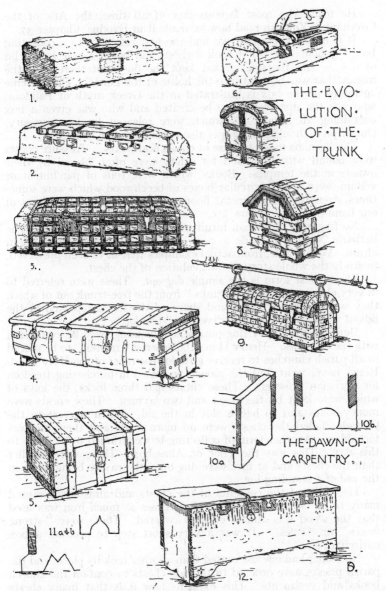

THE·EVO-
LUTION·
OF·THE·
TRUNK

THE·DAWN·OF·
CARPENTRY.

1.
2.
3.
4.
5.
6.
7.
8.
9.
10a.
10b.
11a&b.
12.

CHESTS: DUG-OUT AND SLAB CONSTRUCTIONS.—1. Primitive Dug-out. 2. Saxon
Chest. 3. Perfected Dug-out. 4. Chest at Wimborne. 5. Chest showing
Slab Construction. 6-9. Early Trunks. 10a and 10b. Sides, 11a and 11b.
Feet. 12. Jacobean Chest.

7

He made the most famous box of all time, the Ark of the Covenant. You can read how he made it in Exodus, Chapter 37.

It is in the Bible that we find the first reference to a collecting box, " Jehoida the priest took a chest, and bored a hole in the lid of it . . . and the priests that kept the door put therein all the money that was brought into the house of the Lord." The extreme antiquity of the box is illustrated in the Greek myth of Pandora, who was the first woman to be created and who was given a box containing all human ills which were released by her curiosity. Out of pity, though, Hope was also enclosed in the chest.

The Romans made full use of chests and boxes. Treasure chests were bound with iron, and for safety were often placed by their owners in the temples. Books, which were rolls of parchment or vellum, were kept in circular boxes of beechwood which were sometimes strengthened by metal hoops. These were the ancestors of our band-boxes for collars, etc.

No fragment of Roman furniture in England has survived. The barbaric Northman made a clean sweep. The whole story began afresh. We are able, from actual examples that have been preserved, to study the whole story of the evolution of the chest.

The earliest form is the simple *dug-out*. These were referred to in very old documents as " trunks " from the tree-trunk out of which they were shaped. The round shape of the log is repeated in the lids of what are still called travelling " trunks."

Many of the heavy dug-outs still remaining may be connected with the Crusades. Henry II in 1166 ordered " trunks " to be placed in all parish churches to receive gifts for the relief of the Holy Land. Henry never went, but the money was used in purchasing freedom for Christian prisoners. These chests had three locks, the keys of which were kept by the priest and two laymen. These chests were money-boxes and so had a slot in the lid. When interest in the Crusades faded the chests were no more made and their use was forbidden. Another form of collecting-box continued to be made to this day. This was the Poor or Alms-box. These were smaller than the chests and at first were dug-outs, the cavity being hewn in the *end* of a standing log.

The value of the contents of the chests and alms-boxes caused many to be banded with iron. Sometimes so much iron was used that the wood was almost entirely covered. These were " strong boxes " or " safes." It was a very short step to produce a box entirely of iron.

No sooner had one use ceased than another took its place, and the parish priests were ordered to provide chests to contain the church books and vestments. This explains how it is that many chests have a small division which held the books and parchments and a larger division which held the church vestments, altar cloths, etc.

At this time a great advance was being made in the construction of chests. The awkward " dug-out " was displaced by the " slab construction." Five hewn planks were spiked or pegged together

PLATE V

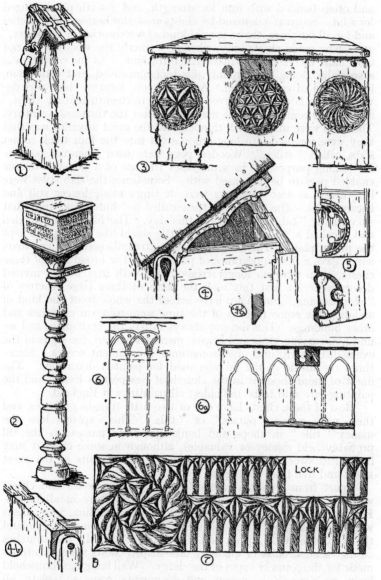

POOR-BOXES AND THIRTEENTH-CENTURY CHEST.—1 and 2. Poor-boxes
3. Thirteenth-Century Chest. 4. 4a and 4b. Hinges. 5. Thirteenth-
Century Decoration of Chest Feet. 6 and 6a. Arcading. 7. Decoration
of a Chest Front.

and often banded with iron for strength, and a sixth plank hinged for a lid. So great a demand for chests arose, for homes and churches and for all purposes, that a special kind of woodworker, a " cofferer," arose who made chests only, whereas formerly the woodworker not only built the house but made the furnishing. As the cofferer was a specialist doing one job only, his tools improved, and with them, his method of construction. A very lovely form of chest was devised which is always referred to as a " thirteenth-century chest," although it continued to be made long after the thirteenth century. The sides were made much thinner, and the great advance was that they were tongued into long grooves cut into the four thick corner slabs called " stiles." Wooden pegs were used wherever possible for joining purposes. In some cases the use of a dovetail tongue enabled pegs to be dispensed with. Sometimes the slab stiles were lengthened as feet and later were at times made longer still and became legs. The chest was then called a " hutch," a word that survives in " rabbit hutch " to this day. The hinge was wooden and is called a " pin hinge," and a little shield-like metal plate kept the pin in place. The ends were often strengthened with crossbars which gave a first appearance of panelling. The broad face of these chests, that were no longer criss-crossed with iron bands, invited decoration. At first this took the form of three large rosettes of " chip carving," but many have across the whole front the kind of arcading the stone masons of the time were using in churches and other buildings. This did not always satisfy the craftsman, and we find him carving birds and beasts, men and women, the signs of the evangelists, scriptural, and sometimes tournament scenes. Sometimes the inside of the lid was used for painted decoration. The finest of these chests is in the church of Newport in Essex, and the paintings are said to be the oldest oil paintings in England.

Most of these chests have one or two little troughs or boxes, and these were called " purses " or " tills." This explains how the money " tills " in shops and banks got their names, as the till probably held money or valuables, although in some cases it may have held sweet-smelling herbs to keep the contents of the chest sweet and free from contagion.

Apart from " church chests," for long years boxes and chests were by far the most important items of furniture in all homes. For storing clothes so that they did not need folding, long chests were made called " garde-robes " in France, although in England the wardrobe stood up on end like a cupboard. In the churches strange semi-circular or quadrangular-shaped chests were sometimes made for the copes or capes of the clergy. Wall hangings, household linen, cushions, beds, papers and documents, coins and plate, all were stored in their own chests (as at Wells, York, etc.). In monasteries books had their own chests or " book-cases." Merchants stored their goods in large, flat-topped trunks called " counters " from the fact that some of their lids were scored like " counter boards " to assist their money counting. Business offices were

PLATE VI

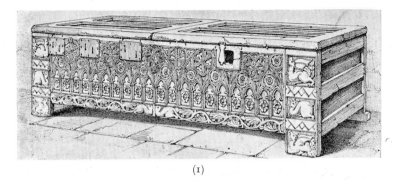

(1)

(3)

(2)

ARCADED CHESTS.—1. Saltwood, Kent. 2. Crediton, Devon. 3. Faversham, Kent.

PLATE VII

(1)

(2)

(3)

FOREIGN CHESTS.—1. East Dereham Chest (Flemish Figure Type). 2. Italian
Carved Chest (Cassone). 3. Tyrolean Cedar-wood Chest.

called " counting-houses " until very recent times. The household linen, clothing and goods that a woman brought as her share at her marriage was kept in her " dower chest," and these were sometimes very magnificent indeed. In Italy these became the finest chests of all. They are called " cassoni " and may be seen in good museums.

It must be remembered that from the time of the Conquest until the time of the Tudors, and even later, all important land-owners, kings, nobles, knights and squires, abbots and bishops were in constant movement from castle to castle, from manor to manor. Furniture, hangings, tapestries, bedding and cushions, armour, liveries and clothing, goods and chattels, all and everything except trestle tables and wall benches was packed into chests, packing cases and travelling trunks and slung upon the backs of sumpter mules and pack-horses. People sat upon the chests by day and slept upon them at night.

Throughout the Middle Ages the cofferers were gaining in skill, and sometime between 1400 and 1450 they began to use a really great invention. We do not know by whom or where the use of the PANEL first took place (viii). Most likely it was introduced to England from Flanders or from France, and probably it was accepted slowly, and no one can receive praise for one of the great inventions of all time. All wood construction was affected by the introduction of the panel. With regard to chests, the front and back were the first parts to be *framed*, then the sides, bottom and lid. The riven oaken slab stiles were exchanged for squared timber, and into these stiles the cross-pieces (rails) were tenoned at top and bottom. So the frame was made by the intelligent use of the mortise-and-tenon joint. The constant use of the word " frame " or " framing " in-dicates its importance. We have mirror and picture frames, door and window frames ; there are frame buildings ; the skeleton con-struction of any wooden object is framing ; there are cold frames in the garden, and frames to our umbrellas, etc. Into grooves in the rails and stiles thin boards (panels) were fitted. By allowing room for the panel to expand or contract the old fear of splitting was lost.

The introduction of the mortise-and-tenon joint and of the panel began one of the great revolutions in craft working. (" Tenon " is from " tenant," the present participle of the French verb " tenir " = to hold. The tenon is the holding part of the joint, just as a tenant holds a house or property.) Furniture could now be made more lightly, the old stiff standardised patterns could be exchanged for an infinite variety of new shapes ; new methods, such as wood-turning, could be used in furniture-making. New ways of de-corating, first the sunken panel, secondly the framework of stiles and rails, and thirdly the edges where the panel met the framework —called " mouldings "—were devised. So it was that " joined " furniture or " joinery " was born. The " joiner " who joined wood by means of joints became quite separate from the " carpenter " who joined wood by nailing or pegging only.

At about the time of the Wars of the Roses there was much trade across the North Sea. Foreign merchants and workmen settled in England. Some were invited by the English sovereigns, some purchased the right to trade, some were refugees from religious persecutions at home. They came from France, from the Low Countries, from Germany. There was a constant passage backwards and forwards of clergymen to and from Italy. All carried their possessions in boxes, chests and coffers. Coffers of spruce and deal—then very rare woods—came from Danzig, wonderfully carven " Flanders chests " came from the Low Countries, chests of cypress wood came from Italy. New ways of construction were learned by the English " joiner." He began to use the " mitre," first in the corner of the panels and, much later, in the framework (viii. 3). Then the form of panel carving called the " linen-fold " was introduced, most likely from France. This is generally supposed to have been used first in church work and to have represented the cloth or veil that was used on the Altar to cover the chalice. Finally, the true " dovetail " joint came to be used, probably from Italy.

The time of the Tudors was of great importance in the history of the woodworker. England had peace from civil war. Trade with the Continent increased. A new nobility was created in place of the old that had largely perished during the Wars of the Roses. It was no louger necessary to live in the old comfortless castles. Nobles and wealthy merchants sent their sons abroad, especially to Italy, to finish their education. These returned full of new ideas. Kings, merchants and landowners invited foreign craftsmen to come and build and decorate the new houses they were building. All this rich incoming of new ideas is reflected in the chests that still remained a most important article of furniture. Portraits were carved upon the panels, often in circles or " roundels." Inlay with coloured woods began, first with native woods, such as box, holly, pear wood, etc., and later with ebony, and when Queen Mary married Philip of Spain the Spanish method of decorating with an inlay of bone or ivory and mother-of-pearl was introduced (viii and ix). During the time of the Tudors (the Renaissance) scholars not only began to study diligently Greek and Roman writings, but artists, architects and craftsmen began to study Greek and Roman ways of building and decorating and to use them in their work. Chest fronts were arcaded with the semicircular Roman arch. The acanthus leaf, long lines of fluting, interlacing strap-work, geometrical panels, and much more became common, and the style that we call " Jacobean " began to be used. The English oak had been used so recklessly for all purposes that it was not so easy to obtain, and furniture-makers found a substitute in walnut. This wood could be glued easily, and, moreover, could be sawn into very thin sheets which could be used in a very beautiful form of decoration that came to England from Holland during Charles the Second's reign. The Dutch wood-craftsmen had brought to great perfection the Venetian art of laying thin sheets of coloured or marked wood over the body of an article—this was VENEERING. This art was carried further.

PLATE VIII

(1)

(2)

(3)

RENAISSANCE CHESTS.—1. Early Seventeenth-century Chest. 2. "None-such" Inlaid Chest. 3. Panelled and Inlaid Chest (Mid-Seventeenth Century).

PLATE IX

(1)

(2)

EVOLUTION OF THE CHEST OF DRAWERS.—1. A " Mule " Chest with inlay.
2. A Chest of Tall Drawers on Legs, with Marquetry Decoration (Seventeenth Century).

Panels and geometrical shapes were filled with veneer cut from coloured wood and other material formed into patterns. When the patterns were geometrical they were called Parquetry. When they formed birds, flowers, etc., it was called Marquetry (ix and frontispiece). This marquetry was first arranged in small panels of flowers, birds, etc., but later was spread over larger areas and is called " endive " or " seaweed " marquetry, from the resemblance to the fern-like leaves of those plants.

The story of the chest has nearly been told. It has continued to be made until to-day. The woodworker keeps his tools in a tool chest. But the all-important place that the chest held in palace and hovel has been taken by the articles told about in the next section.

THINGS TO DO

1. Make a systematic visit to all the churches within reach, and make a complete record, i.e. draw and measure all the old chests, or old poor-boxes or alms-boxes, being particularly careful with any decoration.
2. There are a number of books dealing solely with old chests. Any good library will supply these for study.
3. In the workshop : make a series of models of the various chests, using their original modes of construction. Make specimens of the joints mentioned iu this section. There are plenty of good books on woodwork joints which give working detail.
4. Make a collection of English woods, oak, elm, ash, beech, holly, yew, pear, apple, ivy, sycamore, etc., and read up their uses.
5. Refer back to " Things To Do " at the end of the first section and continue those applicable with this section.
6. What are " hard " woods and " soft " woods ?
7. Take a thin board of even-grained hardwood, or a sheet of oak-faced plywood ; mark on it a series of traceries in historical order, and pierce the patterns, as a " sampler."
8. Design and make a small cabinet in some definite style.

CHAPTER III

THE CHILDREN OF THE CHEST

THE CHEST OF DRAWERS

WHILE the chest had to be carried about it kept its simple box-like shape. So soon as it could remain in one place it was found to be inconvenient. All chests had lids, hinged at the back. The Greeks and Egyptians made boxes with sliding lids, but these were clearly not suited to the chest. The chest could not be made very high, otherwise it would have been impossible to reach the bottom inside. Then, if something at the bottom was required, the whole contents had to be moved. As soon as " framing " was introduced and the use of the panel, it was possible to make a part of the front separately and a small box fitted in which could be pulled out. So the first " drawer " was made. Drawers were first called " tills." It is clear that these were the result of a more settled mode of living. The first drawers had thick sides which were grooved and ran on " bearers," and the fronts and sides were nailed together. This was bad, and by the end of Elizabeth's reign one large dovetail was used. By the time of Queen Anne the common dovetail was in full use in drawer construction, and from then on very beautiful varieties of the dovetail joint were introduced. At first one or two drawers were put in the bottom of a chest, and these are called " mule chests " (ix). The advantage of the drawer over the box led to a very rapid development of the " chest of drawers," until the whole framework of the chest was filled with drawers, and the lid was no longer necessary. The chest of drawers became higher and higher. Sometimes it was raised on a stand, sometimes one set was placed upon another set, and in this way the " tall-boy," which reaches to the ceiling, was born.

Many combinations of chests of drawers with cupboards, etc., have been made, of which there is no space to tell here.

THE CABINET

The invention of the " drawer " solved the difficulty of storing a number of small articles, trinkets, jewellery, writing or toilet requisites, etc., separately, but in the same article of furniture. Chests entirely filled with a nest of small drawers were made in the

14

PLATE X

A MAHOGANY BUREAU, in the form of a Double Chest of Drawers
(Mid-Eighteenth Century).

PLATE XI

(1)   (2)

CLOCK CASES.—1. Decorated with Arabesque Marquetry, *circa* 1700.
2. A Lacquered Case (Early Eighteenth Century).

time of the early Tudors. These chests were usually provided with a pair of doors so that the contents could be protected by one locking operation, and to ensure that the drawers should not tip out when the cabinet was carried from place to place. In order that they should be easily accessible they were, in most cases, supplied with a stand. These chests were called " cabinets." As the cabinet contained articles of value, great care was taken in its construction and decoration. The smallness of the drawer joints and other parts of the cabinets necessitated the use of hardwoods and so the most skilful of woodworkers in hardwoods came to be called cabinet-makers. It was fortunate, too, for the cabinet-makers that a new wood was introduced to Europe that was so well fitted for the purpose. This was MAHOGANY. It seems that the first Englishman to use mahogany was Sir Walter Raleigh, who, on one of his expeditions to the Spanish Main, repaired his ships with the wood. It was being regularly imported by 1715. Its beauty of colour and markings, its freedom from warpiug and twisting, its strength and the fact that it could be used for delicate carving, led to its use for all kinds of furniture. Later on other beautiful woods, one of the chief of which was satin-wood, were used in cabinet-making, and even to-day new woods are continually being used beside the old favourites for gramophone and wireless cabinets.

The chest of drawers and the cabinet are but two of the great family of the " children of the chest." Two others that always deserve attention are the " commode " which is a kind of chest of drawers with a curved front, and very numerous varieties of writing " bureaux."

AN ASSORTMENT OF BOXES

The extraordinary use of the chest in the Middle Ages has been continued to our own times by a very great number of small boxes and cases made for special purposes. There are the letter- and the pillar-boxes, often not boxes at all. There are paint- and pencil-boxes with an ancestry going back to prehistoric Egypt. The solicitor's deed-boxes and the business man's cash-box are direct descendants of the small chests containing valuable documents that were left for safe-keeping in the churches, and the iron-bound coffer that was kept at the foot of the feudal lord's bed. Tinder-boxes gave way to match-boxes. Snuff-boxes, still occasionally used, were often exquisite little masterpieces. Books and boxes have always been closely related. The Romans had a special kind of chest for books called a " scrinium," and the " shrine," which is a chest for sacred things, was used in the Irish Church for preserving the Sacred Writings. The Scandinavian word to-day for a small box is " skrin." In Portestant England the scriptures were preserved in Bible-boxes. Bookbinders at first used thin wooden " boards " for book-covers, and the modern substitute is called " *cardboard* " and the outer binding of a book is its " case." Portable writing-desks which open with a sloping surface for writing

2 *

PLATE XII

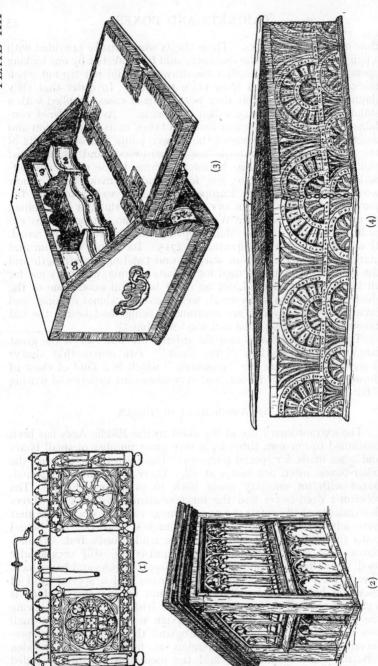

SMALL BOXES.—1. Casket.   2. Desk and Book-box (Mediæval).   3. Writing Desk, *circa* 1700 A.D.   4. Bible-box, Jacobean.

purposes, and which contain a variety of small compartments, have been made from the time of the Renaissance until to-day. For the special accommodation of articles of attire there have been lace, glove, collar, hat and glove boxes, etc.

Perhaps the best known of boxes made for special purposes are tea-caddies. The word is an English form of a Malay word meaning a weight of one-and-a-third pounds used in the measurement of tea. Tea did not come into common use until the last years of Cromwell. Tea was then from £5 to £10 a pound. It never became a really cheap article, and at one time (1810) tea duty was as much as 2s. 2¼d. per pound. No wonder it was kept under lock and key. A pound of tea in a suitable casket was an acceptable present among the very well-to-do. The key of the caddy was kept by the mistress of the house. Beautiful little boxes were made by the most skilful craftsmen and reflected the style of ornament in vogue at the time. The first tea came from China only, and so the earliest caddies were small, and have but one compartment. Much later, at about 1838, tea was also imported from India, and so caddies were made with two compartments, one for China and one for India tea. A third compartment was sometimes added for the white loaf sugar which was too expensive an item to be left as an open temptation to children or servants. The introduction of tea was accompanied with cups (the first of which had no handles) and saucers, teapots, bowls and jugs of china ware, and corner cupboards and china cabinets were devised for their safe-keeping. Special tea-tables also were made. Special fast vessels called clippers were built for the China trade, and, besides tea, brought home, among other things, lacquered articles. This form of decorating wooden articles became extremely popular, and for nearly a hundred years after Wlliam and Mary came to the throne, very much furniture was decorated with lacquer.

At about the same time that tea-caddies began to be made, another old friend, the grandfather's clock, made its appearance. There had been clocks for many years, but the great invention of the pendulum made it possible to produce exact time-keepers at a low cost. The practical use of the pendulum is due to a Dutchman, Huygens, in 1657, the same year that the first tea-shop was opened in London. Charles II was then in exile in Holland and acquired a collector's mania for clocks. Under his patronage the clock-makers of London became famous. Glass faces, boxes to preserve the works from dust, and long bodies to enclose the weights and pendulum were made. These were raised upon a foot or pedestal for steadiness, and the three part " grandfather " clock case was made.

Finally, in this very incomplete notice of the uses of boxes must be mentioned the knife-boxes that were made at much the same time as tea-caddies and clock-cases. Up to William III's time it was a general custom for men to carry their own knives. Forks were unknown except as a rarity for the eating of fruit. The intro-duction of the fork from Italy in Stuart times was preached against as disrespect to God—the proverb says, " Fingers were made before forks "—and those particular folk who wished to use forks carried them about in small cases. Manners improved slowly, and guests carried cases with knife, fork and spoon, just as soldiers on active service do to-day. Then the custom arose of the wealthy purchasing sets for their personal use and that of favoured guests. These were valuable and were kept locked in knife-boxes which had a place of honour on the sideboard of the dining-room. Nowadays their place has been taken in some degree by "canteens " of cutlery.

CUPBOARDS

Boxes have lids. Place a box on end and the *lid* becomes a *door* and the *box* a *cupboard*.

Fix a door to a hole in a wall and one has a " built-in " cupboard. These can sometimes be found in old churches. In old farm-houses and inns there were similar cupboards in the thickness of the wall beside the fireplace in which spices, etc., were kept. To-day it is a frequent custom to fit cupboards, wardrobes, bookcases, etc., into recesses.

We have seen that the chest was sometimes raised from the floor and that it was then called a " hutch " (xxxi). Its lid could then serve the purpose of a " table," but when it was in use as a table the lid could not be raised, and so doors were necessary. The rabbit " hutch " in the backyard is most often a box with a door.

There are so many varieties of cupboards, and of combinations of the cupboard with the shelf, or of the cupboard and the drawer, that it is best to speak of them with regard to the main use to which they were put. They serve—

1. in connection with food and drink ;
2. in connection with clothes ;
3. in connection with books, documents or writing materials ;
4. for the safe keeping of valuables.

Dealing first with section 1 we can draw up a sort of family tree of the principal members of the family (see p. 20).

The story can be told very simply. From the rough board or plank the woodworker in the castle-yard could fashion a chest or a shelf upon which drinking horns and wooden bowls, etc., could be placed, and which became the cupboard or the table top. The chest, we have seen, became a " hutch " with doors instead of a lid (although often a chest raised upon legs or a stand is called a hutch). The hutch was lengthened upwards and a shelf or shelves placed in it. This was called an AUMBRY, and was the ancestor of all true cupboards.

In churches many aumbries were placed to act as " dole cupboards " which contained the bread that was distributed to the poor. In domestic use the aumbries have an interesting story. In the great houses the important retainers and officials soon ceased to sleep in the Great Hall. They received separate rations of food,

PLATE XIII

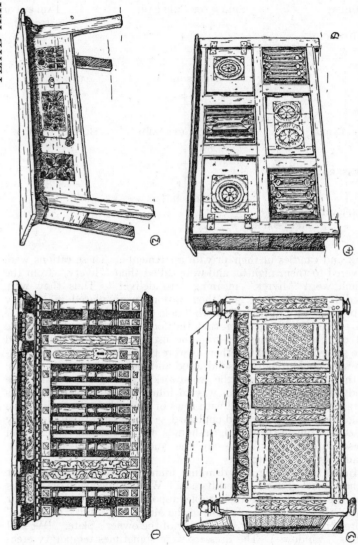

HUTCHES AND CUPBOARDS.—1. Alms Cupboard (St. Alban's Abbey) (Seventeenth Century). 2. The Ancestor of the Sideboard (Mediæval). 3. Livery Cupboard (Jacobean). 4. A Cupboard (Fifteenth Century).

19

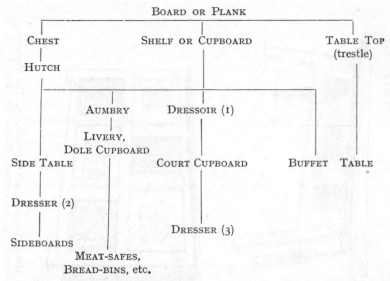

BOARD OR PLANK

CHEST	SHELF OR CUPBOARD	TABLE TOP (trestle)
HUTCH		
	AUMBRY DRESSOIR (1)	
	LIVERY, DOLE CUPBOARD	
SIDE TABLE		COURT CUPBOARD BUFFET TABLE
DRESSER (2)		
		DRESSER (3)
SIDEBOARDS		
MEAT-SAFES, BREAD-BINS, etc.		

drink and candles in their private apartments. These rations were delivered to them nightly, and were called their " livery," from the French word " livrer," meaning " to deliver." Thus they were called livery servants, and their rations were placed in " livery cupboards " or " liveries." Both " dole cupboards " and " liveries " had pierced fronts in order that the food should keep fresh. The first of these were made before the use of joints was known and were spiked or pegged together, as were the early chests. The openings were cut through the solid wood and looked like little windows. As the stone mason and the woodworker grew further apart, the woodworker sought his own way of filling in the framework of his doors, and this he often did with rows of turned spindles which gave a cage-like effect to his food cupboards. These can still occasionally be seen in out-of-the-way farm-houses and are called " bread and cheese cupboards." These are the ancestors of our meat-safes, bread-bins, larders, etc.

In all ages eating and drinking utensils have been the subject of the utmost skill of the craftsman. Wealthy people have always used the splendour of their table appointments to indicate their riches. In the noblemen's halls of the Middle Ages tall " dressoirs," or dressers, were built for the display of the owner's plate. (We still " dress " windows.) The dressers were sometimes temporary erections of shelves taken down after the occasion for their use was over, or when the lord went on his travels. Gradually they became very splendid pieces of permanent furniture with cupboards below, shelves above and crowned with a canopy. The whole was enriched with carving, painting or gilding and sometimes with coloured cloths.

The hutch also continued to develop. The top was lengthened and used as a side table for serving purposes. These proved to be so useful that they gave rise to two types of furniture. In the first, the hutch was omitted and the true TABLE was born (xiii). In the second the drawer took the place of the cupboard or hutch, and the kind of " dresser," which was really a long side-table or sideboard furnished with a line of drawers, was made. The skilled furniture-makers of later days took the three units, the (1) broad table for display, (2) drawers for storing table napery, (3) cupboards for storing food or drink, and from them made an infinite variety of sideboards, etc.

Returning for a moment to the manor house. With an advance in the comfort of living the family withdrew from the hall and lived and drank in more private apartments. Two new forms of furniture were evolved to suit the new mode of living. One was the " court cupboard " that is always associated with Tudor times (xiv and xxxi). It probably received its name from the French word " court," meaning " short," in comparison with the lordly dresser in the hall. The other was the " buffet." The court cupboard was used for storing food, drink, and utensils. The buffet was used for display and possibly service. The latter is interesting as some people regard the picturesquely dressed Tudor servitor or " buffetier " who tended the buffet as supplying the name to the " beef-eater," as the Royal Yeomen of the Guard are vulgarly called, who retain the livery of the time of their formation, the accession of Henry VII in 1485.

" Last scene of all, that ends this strange, eventful history," the dresser reappeared again in its original form, not in the baronial hall or regal palace, but in the yeoman's farm, in parsonages, and finally in the artisan's and labourer's cottages. It had the cupboard at the base and the shelves above, and sometimes a drawer or so midway. Its shelves did not display the gold and silverware of the noble but gleamed with pewter and was bright with " willow pattern " china. One refinement it did borrow sometimes from the houses of the well-to-do was glass doors as a protection against dust.

A second use of cupboards and cupboard-like furniture is for storing clothes. The first question to ask in looking at an old piece of furniture is, " What purpose did it serve ? " Only when we see how perfectly that purpose is served, how the wood was chosen, how the construction was adapted to the wear and tear of daily use, how well it fitted the place for which it was designed, can we consider the means by which it was made pleasant to the eye, that is, its decoration.

Clothes are continually changing. They differ according to country and region, according to rank, position or occupation, and according to time. Furniture reflects the nature of clothes worn. If every one took to wearing shirts and shorts nine-tenths of our wardrobes would become unnecessary.

In early and mediæval days clothes were simple and few. The worker needed no store, he possessed but one suit, mainly the one-piece garment he stood in. The shopkeeper and parson and such people added a washable under-garment, a " shift," so called because it could be changed and washed. The gentry were easily able to store their spare wear in chests, and these tended to get longer as time went on so that cloaks need not to be folded. Large chests called " standards " were made for spare clothes and for retainers' liveries when travelling. The continual travelling of well-to-do people to-day gives much employment to makers of dressing-cases, travelling trunks, etc. We have seen how clothes chests were made for church vestments, altar clothes. It is likely that the earliest clothes *cupboards* or wardrobes are to be found in churches. There is a very famous one in Chester Cathedral, of which parts are perhaps as old as 1295, the year in which Edward I summoned the " first complete and model parliament."

The word " press " was used from very early times with reference to aumbries, but came to mean two quite separate kinds of furniture. There are (1) cider and cheese presses, trouser and book printers' presses, etc., and (2) large cupboards used for storing purposes. We should call clothes presses wardrobes to-day. These usually have a large upper portion in which clothes can be hung, together with drawers, trays or cupboard compartments for storing smaller articles. The large doors gave a splendid scope for the marquetry worker and for the display of beautifully figured veneers. The panels of these large pieces of furniture are always well worth study as they show so well the difference of treatment that is possible with different woods.

The third use for cupboards and such-like pieces of furniture is for storing books, documents and writing materials. Very early illuminated manuscripts show three ways of storing books, (1) the chest, (2) the aumbry, (3) sloping shelves with a curtain in front. In places where books were constantly in use the shelf was by far the best arrangement (in monasteries, churches and schools). As books were rare and valuable they were chained, and this made it necessary for a sloping writing shelf to be provided for students below the book-shelves. Some of these combination book- and writing-shelves are to be seen in cathedrals and the older colleges of universities.

It was not until long after the introduction of printing that private people began to have sufficient books to require more than a shelf or a chest for their accommodation. One of the first references we have of bookcases being made to order were those for Samuel Pepys in 1666, the year of the Great Fire of London, who said that at one time he had so many books that he had to give some away. At the same time Sir Christopher Wren gave much thought to the fitting of libraries. Their master, Charles II, was interested in science and founded the Royal Society. It became fashionable for every great house to have its library. This was a fine opportunity for the cabinet-makers. Larger and larger bookcases were made.

PLATE XIV

(2)

(1)

1. SIDEBOARD (Late Tudor).   2. COURT CUPBOARD (Jacobean).

PLATE XV

(2)

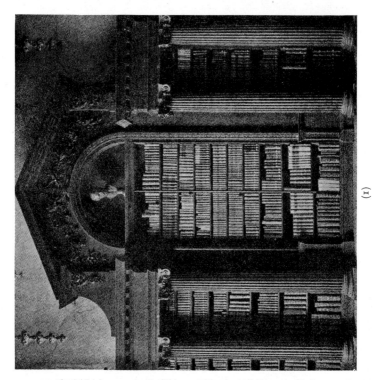

(1)

BOOKCASES.—1. An " Architectural " Bookcase, from Christ Church Library, Oxford (Palladian, Mid-Eighteenth Century).
2. The Bookcase as a Piece of Furniture (Late Eighteenth Century).

Some of these bookcases, because of their absolute fitness to purpose, the perfection of their cabinet work, their strength coupled with their perfect proportion—one must always bear in mind the great weight of a large number of books—and the careful use of ornament, neither too much nor too little but just enough to indicate that the case contained something precious, all this made some of these bookcases among the finest products of the English furniture-maker's workshops.

The only improvements of recent years has been an attempt to avoid the awkwardness of large glazed doors in small rooms. Sliding doors, and sectional doors to lift up and run in over the top of the books, have been introduced.

THINGS TO DO

1. Start a collection of drawings of joints, making especial note of the *uses* to which they are put.
2. In the workshop, start to *make* a collection of joints.
3. Make a series of drawings of panels, giving details of the mouldings in historical order.
4. Whenever opportunity offers add to your collection of sketches decorative details of panels and of the framing of panels.
5. Begin a collection of drawings of furniture taken from illuminated manuscripts. An increasing number of these are being introduced into history books, particularly books on Social History. (For instance, the excellent series of books on Everday Life in Prehistoric Times, in Greece and Rome, and in England, by Marjorie and C. H. B. Quennell.) Remember that these drawings may not be true in construction, as the artists were not woodworkers.
6. Start a notebook of historical facts that influenced furniture-making. Make entries of books (giving full titles) where you read any interesting fact about furniture or see a good picture (give page and enter the nature of the picture or detail).

CHAPTER IV

THE CHAIR

Thus saith the Lord, The heaven is My throne, and the earth is My footstool.

PRIMITIVE man sat on the ground. At the present day it is probable that the vast majority of mankind use the same seat. The ruler, the chieftain or headsman, may sit upon a throne or chair of state, but his people either stand in his presence or sit on the ground. For long ages the chair was a symbol of authority rather than an article of use and comfort. In all formal business to-day the leader " takes the chair," becomes " chairman," and all remarks have to be addressed to " the chair." In old days a person who was honoured was " chaired." At Bisley the champion rifle shot, the King's Prizeman, is chaired by his supporters. In mediæval schools the schoolmaster sat while his scholars kneeled before him or sat on benches. In Universities to-day we speak of the Professors as occupying " chairs " of philosophy, chemistry, history, and the like. In the two houses of Parliament there is but one Chair—The Speaker's Chair, which with its dais and canopy is a true example of the mediæval seigniorial chair.

The " throne " takes first place among chairs in both Church and State. In all cathedrals the Bishop's seat is called a throne. Cathedral is derived from the Latin word " cathedra," meaning a chair. The cathedral is the seat-place of a Bishop. We speak of country houses of wealthy people as being " seats."

Just as with chests and tables, the Egyptians perfected chair-making thousands of years before the beginning of civilisation in England. Chair and bed legs, carved in the form of ox legs, and having perfect tenons, have been found dating from at least 400 B.C. The very earliest wall-paintings show the gods seated upon a square box-like seat with a low back. Almost as soon we see a perfect chair with four animal-shaped legs and no stretchers. Stools of all kinds appear, especially one with crossed legs exactly like our camp stools. Chair-making became a fine art, and for lightness of construction combined with strength and grace of outline have probably never been beaten. The art of chair-making spread to the Mediterranean countries and kept its excellence in both Greece and Italy.

PLATE XVI

(2)

(1)

SEATS WITH CANOPIES.—1. Stalls at All Saints, Hereford.   2. French Canopied Seat (both Fifteenth Century).

PLATE XVII

(1)

(2)

(3)

(4)

MISERICORDS AND CANOPY.—1 and 2. Misericords from St. Nicholas, King's Lynn.   3. Misericord from Norwich Cathedral
4. Detail of the Canopies of the Stalls in All Saints, Hereford (see Plate XVI), (all Fifteenth-Century).

It was to the north though, rather than to the south, that England owes its seating arrangements. The set-out of the Scandinavian and Saxon hall was followed in England in both church and manor. There was a raised seat for the Lord, Abbot or Bishop, and fixed wall benches running round for lesser folk. In mediæval England these were supplemented by chests, forms and stools. The "high seat" in Scandinavia was flanked by two richly carven wooden pillars. The isolation of the "high seat" caused the raised platform to be extended, forming a dais so that members of the family and honoured guests could be accommodated. The seat itself was sometimes extended and provided with a back and a canopy. The latter was not only an indication of rank but was a protection against draughts and leaky roofs.

Chairs are either (1) the leg type or (2) the box type. That is, they descend either from the three-legged stool or from the chest.

The Leg Type

The simplest form of this is the three-legged milking stool or the old-fashioned butcher's block. The leg is driven into a hole of approximately the same size and wedged in, as the hammer-head is wedged on to the handle. This method was used in a kind of chair that probably came from Norway and which was made down to Tudor times ; it was used for Windsor chairs and for spindle and ladder-back chairs, and is used for kitchen chairs, etc., to-day.

The Box Type

People sat on chests. By adding a back and sides an early kind of chair was formed, the lid of the chest being the seat of the chair. So soon as the chest was "framed" by using the tenon joint, it was possible to omit the solid sides and one has the beginning of the modern chair.

The two ways of making furniture led to very bitter feeling between the carpenters and the joiners. Workmen of the same craft have always joined to look after their own interests. There were craft Guilds in Roman times. We do not know how early woodworkers in England began to form Guilds. As early as Henry V (who fought at Agincourt) there were in London Guilds of Cofferers and Carpenters. It was a serious offence for the member of one craft to undertake work that belonged to another. The turners (who used the lathe), the joiners and the carpenters were continually quarrelling. In Charles the Second's time an effort was made to put a stop to this, and the following extract is taken from the attempted agreement :—

That these workes next following doe pperly (properly) belong to the Joyners.

. . . . 2. Item all sorts of chayres and stooles which are made with mortesses and tennants

. . . . 4. Item all sorts of formes framed made of boards with the sides pinned or Glued.

. . . . 5. Item all sorts of Chests being framed duftalled or Glued. . . .

3

PLATE XVIII

OLD CHAIRS.—1. Dunmow Chair (Thirteenth Century). 2. Turned Chair (Late Sixteenth Century). 3. The Coronation Chair (Mediæval). 4. A "Glastonbury" Collapsible Chair (Jacobean).

PLATE XIX

(1) (2)

(3) (4)

1 and 2. POPPY HEADS, from Ludlow, Shropshire, and Gresford, Denbigh.   3 and 4. STALL
ELBOWS, from Chester Cathedral, and The Carpenter, from Amiens.

PLATE XX

(1)

(2)

(3)

(4)

BENCH-ENDS.—1. From Lapford, Devon, with Renaissance influence. 2. Flamboyant Tracery, from Jarrow, Durham.   3. Perpendicular, from Fressingfield, Suffolk. 4. From St. Mary the Virgin, Wiggenhall, Norfolk.

And these works following doe properlie belong to the Carpenter.
. . . . 2. Item . . . all . . . Stooles whatsoever that are to be headed
with Oake Elme Beeche or Deal and footed with square or
round feet Except all framed stooles glued or pinned. . . .

From this it is clear that the joiner might not use nails, but
was confined to framing, pinning (with wooden pins or dowels) and
glueing, while the carpenter might not use joints. Chairs, forms,
stools for the dairy, wash-house, kitchen, or workshop were carpenter's work ; articles for the " best rooms " were joiner's work.

THE CHAIR AND SEATING IN CHURCHES

Even during the fiercest Civil War the property of the Church
was usually respected. Abbots and important Prelates might
travel from manor to manor, but the monks remained stationary in
monastery and priory. Their occupations required permanent seating arrangements. No human body could stand the strain of con-
tinuous services starting at midnight and lasting till sunset, day in
and day out for a lifetime, without sitting down at times. Our
oldest chairs are all connected with churches.

In the south wall of the sanctuary of many churches there are
seats built in the thickness of the wall for the use of the clergy.
They are usually arranged step-like to indicate the rank of the priests
and are called sedilia, the plural of the Latin " sedile," meaning
" a seat." Another kind of chair is often seen in the sanctuary,
a chair with X legs which was used by important visiting clergy.
This chair really belongs to a third kind of chair which could be
taken apart, or would fold up, and so could be transported easily.
Chairs of this kind were called " fald-stools," i.e. folding stools.

Next to the sanctuary came the choir. In the unheated,
draughty, and sometimes leaky churches, the monks had to be
sheltered as much as possible, and so the seats were given backs
and canopies and sides. A special kind of seat was required.
The monk might sit during sermon, but he had to stand when taking
part in the service. Services were long and numerous, and sometimes the monks were old or infirm. The seats were hinged, and
when lifted, a large bracket underneath gave support, so that the
monk could rest in a semi-standing yet perfectly devout position
with his arms on the broad surface of the division between stall and
stall, an excellent position for chanting. These bracket seats are
called " misereres " or " misericords " from Latin words meaning
" to have mercy " or " pity." The carvings on the brackets are
an important source of information as to the life and customs, the
clothing and occupations of the times. One may see people at work
and play, fighting or hunting, there are strange beasts and strange
men, Biblical scenes, and scenes representing the seasons. It is
always well worth while to lift these misericords, for they have much
to tell. These seats running round the sides of the choir resemble

3 *

the fixed wall benches of the manor halls, except that each seat is separate ; lt is a " stall," just as there are stalls in stables, and in theatres. The carviug of the stalls did not cease with the misericord. The canopies became miracles of craft-work that were repeated in the font covers in many churches. Bands of carving ran around the backs of the stalls, the hand-holds are always worth notice, while the end of the last stall and the front of the first line of stalls gave splendid spaces for carver's work. The end of each line of stalls was often crowned with what is called a " poppy head." The older spelling is " popey head " and is derived from the French word " poupé," meaning a doll, from the fact that the subject chosen was frequently a small human figure, although foliage, strange beasts, angels, and many other subjects were chosen.

In the body of the church the only seating provided at first was an occasional stone bench against the walls for the aged or in-firm. These are still to be seen in some porches. Every one went to church, and the gentry soon separated themselves from the commoners and partitions were erected which screened them from the public view. These partitioned places were raised from off the cold stone floors and were called " pews," from a Latin word meaning an elevated place. They were provided with seats and in some cases became comfortable little rooms. Rent was paid for these box pews and sometimes the whole church was filled with them. Poorer people sat on benches, and the bench-ends were often carved in the same manner as the stall-ends of the choir.

THE CHAIR IN THE HOME

As a separate, movable piece of furniture, the chair was slow to develop in England. Except for very rare " fald-stools " the forms, stools, benches and chests served the rough life of the times. A man in armour needed something substantial to sit on. Dangerous times made it safer for a man to sit with his back to the wall, unless he had an armed servant to stand and guard his back.

There was greater security and luxury in the trading cities of the Low Countries, and so chair-making developed there, and the Flanders chair was imported to England at the end of the fourteenth century. This had a solid framed box-like base with solid arms and back. By Henry VIII's time men no longer needed to wear armour, life in the houses of the wealthy became more comfortable, and chairs began to be more common. The lower part of the panelling began to be left out, leaving four independent legs with connecting bottom rails called " stretchers." The stretchers were either right on the floor or but slightly raised above it. The front stretcher was a " foot-rest " used to keep the feet off the cold, draughty stone floor. The front legs were " turned " or " thrown " by the wood-turner, and, so soon as the stretchers were raised a short distance from the floor, the end of the legs began to be shaped as feet. The backs were still solid from the seat upward.

PLATE XXI

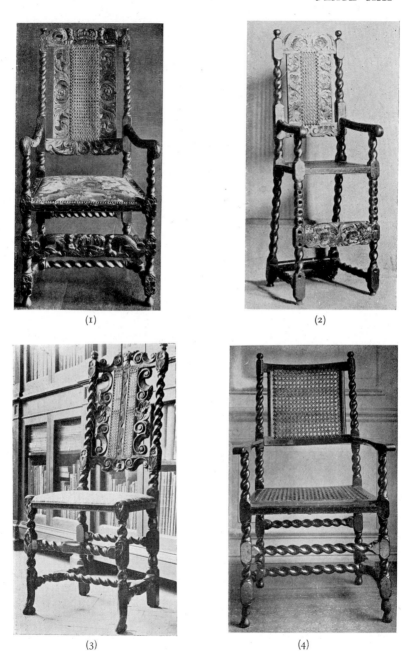

(1)   (2)

(3)   (4)

" RESTORATION " CHAIRS.—1. Single-panel Cane Back. 2. Child's High Chair.
3. Double-panel Cane Back. 4. Cane Seat and Back.

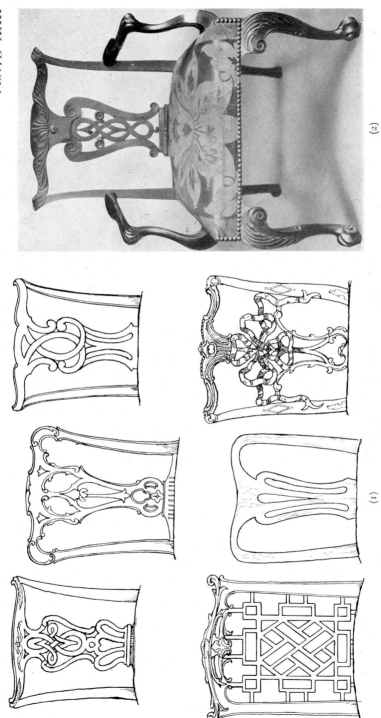

PLATE XXII

(2)

(1)

CHIPPENDALE.—1. Various Backs. 2. Mahogany Chair, *circa* 1750.

The top of the back or " cresting " was often carved elaborately, and sometimes extended beyond the sides and was supported by carved brackets or " ears."

These are the points to be studied in a chair :—

1. How it is put together, remembering the constant strain to which a chair is subjected.
2. The legs, (a) their shape, taking first the front and then the back pair ; (b) their feet ; (c) their stretchers, if there are any, whether plain, turned or carved.
3. The seat, whether wooden, upholstered, or caned or made for a cushion.
4. The back, whether solid or pierced. The shape of the top, if the back is pierced ; the nature of the filling is important.
5. The kind of decoration given to parts of the frame-turning, inlay, veneer, carving, lacquer, paint or gilding, metal mounts or needlework or canework.
6. The kind (or kinds) of wood used.

The solid panel-backed chairs were made until the end of the Commonwealth. They were still most obviously important pieces of furniture, they were master's chair, whether the master were head of the family, Master of a Guild or City Company, whether he were Lord of the Manor or Master of a School or College. Other kinds of chairs were beginning to be made for special purposes in wealthy houses. Light chairs with straight backs, called " gossiping ". chairs, were made for the lady's withdrawing room. Then Queen Elizabeth set the fashion of wearing enormously spread skirts or farthingales and " farthingale " chairs with no arms had to be made so that ladies could sit down. James I had an ill-shapen body and wore padded clothes to hide his deformity. Luxuriously up-holstered furniture with deep cushions and heavy fringes had a passing vogue.

Then came the Civil War between Charles and the Parliament, putting a temporary stop to chair-making as to other things and when the war was over everything for a while was controlled by the serious-minded Puritans and the luxury-loving Cavaliers were either dead or in exile. The chairs, either made at home or imported from the Low Countries, were not decorated, except for a little turning, and had plain leather backs and seats. Wood-turning does not seem to have offended the Puritan eye, and about this time the most difficult work of all, the " barley-sugar twist " was perfected. Two new materials, also, were being introduced. The one was WALNUT wood, and the other rattan CANE, which was most likely introduced by the East India Company (xxii).

Then Charles II came back in 1660. He loved beautiful things. The decorator was encouraged and not restrained. Walnut could be carved across the grain and pierced in a way that was impossible with oak. Beautiful chairs were made with tall backs and seats filled with net-like canework, with sides, cresting and the front

PLATE XXIII

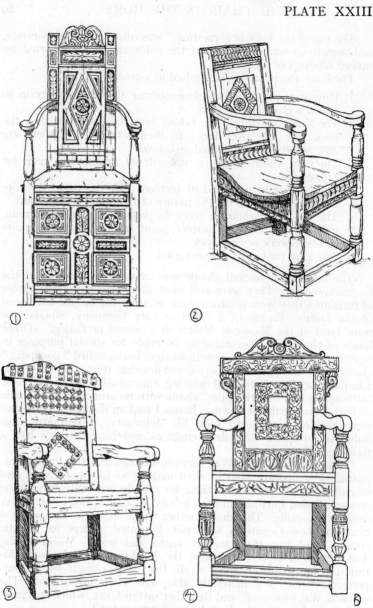

PANEL-BACK CHAIRS.—1. French Enclosed Chair. 2. With Framed Back
(Wareham, Dorset). 3. With Crested Top-piece. 4. With " Ear-
pieces " (Aveley, Essex), (all Early Seventeenth Century).

stretcher elaborately carved. Instead of canework, the back was filled sometimes with " slats," and when these slats were arranged crosswise instead of up and down the chair is called a " ladder-back."

William and Mary's reign was not very happy. William was a foreigner and not popular, and after Mary's death, people were doubtful as to who would succeed him. Chair-makers seem to have reflected this sober spirit. Much decoration left their work although they were busy experimenting. They introduced a curved leg in front instead of the straight up-and-down leg. The chair was beginning to forget its " box " ancestry. Another experiment took the stretchers *diagonally* across, so that people had room for their feet.

All this change and experimenting settled very quickly during the short reign of Queen Anne (from 1702-1714). Very beautiful and restful walnut chairs were made. The stretchers were simplified, and the maker found that his construction was so good that they could be dispensed with altogether. The curved front leg took the delightful shape called the " cabriole," a French word derived from the Latin " caper," meaning a goat. This shape was used in Egypt, Greece and Rome, and it may have been some copying of old forms that led to its use in France and its introduction to England. The origin of the shape as an animal's leg usually shows in the feet, which are often in the form of a flattened hoof and sometimes are the well-known " ball and claw." All the elaborate carving of Charles II's chairs went, and the back became just a frame enclosing one broad splat. One most important change was introduced. Chair-makers seemed at last to realise that people's backs were not straight as a poker but were curved, and that a chair, in order to be comfortable, should have a shaped back. A great change also was coming over social life. No longer was the master of the house the only person who sat upon a chair. An " arm-chair " was still provided for him, but stools, forms and benches became more and more the furniture of schools, inns, chapels and such places, and in the homes of the well-to-do chairs without arms were beginning to be *made in sets* for the family and guests.

Four facts make the years we are now approaching memorable in the history of English chair-making :—

1. Trade was making England a rich country.
2. This wealth enabled people to travel and to see the work of foreign craftsmen.
3. English craftsmen, under the leadership of a succession of master workmen and designers, attained the highest craft skill.
4. The regular importation of mahogany after 1715 gave the chair-makers a wood which enabled them to carry out their designs to the full.

For a time the English designer was strongly influenced by French work, just as the French worker was influenced by Italian

work. In England the Hanoverian Georges had little taste or influence in furniture-making, but in France this was patronised by
a powerful Royal Court. The French sovereigns were no longer
satisfied with the lack of comfort in the mediæval castles. They
built new and splendid palaces, the most marvellous of which is
at Versailles. These needed furnishing. Cabinet-makers were engaged from neighbouring countries. Workshops were established
in the Royal Palace itself. Cost was no object. It is no wonder
that French furniture became a source of inspiration and that
English craftsmen were continually influenced by it.

Wealthy English nobles, land-owners and merchants were also
finding the old manor houses inconvenient places in which to live.
They engaged architects to plan and build new houses. These
studied the Greek and Roman styles of building. The new houses
needed new furniture, and architects and master craftsmen borrowed
Greek and Roman forms of decoration, and even the shapes of chairs
and couches.

Then it chanced that the French came into close contact with
Egypt—Napoleon invaded the country—and Egyptian ways of
decoration and furniture construction became fashionable in France
and England.

Mixed with all these was the strong influence from China, of
which we have spoken.

A new kind of workman also was entering the workshops. All
kinds of schools were becoming common, and almost all intelligent
artisans could read and write. Printing had become common and
cheap, and a new kind of book was appearing. For the first time
craftsmen and designers, mainly in London, were writing about
furniture-making and design, and two kinds of people bought the
books eagerly, the gentlemen in the country, who wished their new
furniture to be in the fashion, and the master woodworkers in the
country workshops, who wished to keep up-to-date.

All this makes a study of chairs while the four Georges sat on
the throne one of constant change and sometimes of bewildering
variety.

Thomas Chippendale, the best known of all English chair-makers,
was born four years after George I came to England, and died at
the age of sixty-one (1718-1779). Probably the son of a Yorkshire
village carpenter, he came to London, and in 1754 made his firm's
name by publishing the first of the books mentioned above. It was
called "The Gentlemen and Cabinet-Maker's Directory," and so
was addressed both to those who ordered and to those who made
furniture. This famous book brought Chippendale to the notice
of wealthy people, and he was soon able to act as managing director
of his business rather than as a working cabinet-maker. At first
he followed every fashion that arose, although his work was always
distinguished by exquisite craftsmanship and strength of construction. The extraordinary imagination of his drawings was always
toned down by his practical common sense when the work was under

PLATE XXIV

(1) (2)

(3) (4)

WILLIAM AND MARY, AND QUEEN ANNE CHAIRS.—1. Ornately Carved Back.
2. Walnut, with Cabriole Legs (Dutch). 3. Lacquered Chair, *circa* 1710.
4. Without Stretcher or Rails.

PLATE XXV

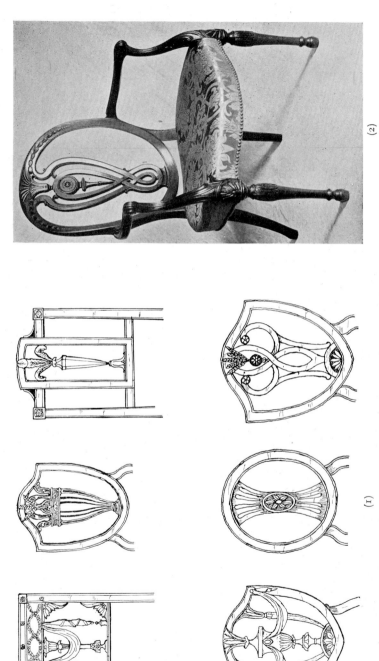

(2)

(1)

HEPPLEWHITE.—1. Various Backs.   2. Oval-back Chair (late Eighteenth Century).

the chisel and plane. He used mahogany almost exclusively for his work. The features we usually remember most with regard to his designs for chairs are the wonderful originality and variety of his designs for the " splat," and the fact that whatever the shape or decoration his chairs all stand firmly as if capable of long hard service.

His work brought him to the notice of a famous Scotch architect, Robert Adam, who had studied in Italy, and who was engaged in building and rebuilding gentlemen's houses. Adam believed that the whole of the house was the architect's business, down to the decoration and the furnishing, and he engaged Chippendale to carry out many of his furniture schemes. Much of the work that we definitely know was carried out by Chippendale's firm was designed or influenced by Adam.

Nine years after Chippendale died, and while his firm was carrying on under his son, another book was published under the name of George Hepplewhite. We know very little about this man, and he had been dead two years before his book was printed. The book was almost entirely influenced by Robert Adam, and shows a development from the substantial Chippendale type to a very much lighter and simpler treatment. Chairs had lost their " square " appearance, backs became gracefully rounded and curved, and, above all, *satin-wood*, which had been introduced somewhere about 1760, began to challenge the sole use of mahogany.

Another rather strange character, Thomas Sheraton, overlapped Chippendale and Hepplewhite, dying in 1806. He came from Stockton-on-Tees in Durham, and settled in London when he was forty years old. He had probably been a journeyman cabinet-maker, but in London made a living by teaching drawing, designing furniture for the trade, and writing books, partly on furniture, partly on religious subjects. He designed extremely graceful chairs. He rejected heavy carving and exaggerated forms but employed a straightness of the back, a breadth of seat and a straight leg in front so that his chairs combine grace with a strength of construction that fitted them for general use. To this he added very delicate ornament, " fluting " and " reeding " arms and legs, and using sometimes the delightful inlay that is always associated with his name.

Returning for a moment to France, we know that the Revolution there swept away all old customs, and that Napoleon emerged from the chaos and finally established himself as Emperor in 1804. The new military Empire vied in splendour with the old French Kingdom. The Court was filled with figures in resplendent uniforms. Furniture was produced to give an effective background to this display. Profuse use was made of gilding and of applied gilt metal ornaments. It is especially interesting that this late development of furniture-making returned for inspiration to the earliest we have mentioned, to the Egyptian and to the Roman. Just as depicted in the Egyptian tomb paintings, chair backs were given a comfortable slope and a roll over at the top, while the legs were given the delicate outward curve of Greek and Roman designs. A reflection of this style came to England and is most commonly seen in the form of inlaying in brass which had a short vogue.

After Sheraton died, in 1806, the spirit seemed to go from furniture designing. The splendidly skilled craftsmen continued to produce mahogany furniture that often is superb in workmanship, and, in suitable surroundings, is sometimes very fine indeed. It is always rather heavy in appearance, it is very heavy to move. The polish is usually beyond all praise, but no effort was made at relief by inlay, and the uniformly dark shade of mahogany does not suit our modern taste for sunlit rooms and happy colours. This has been generally recognised, and the present is a time of change and experiment. Some chair-makers study all old types, and by choosing and adapting these are attempting to satisfy our modern needs, while others say boldly that there is no need to worry about old ways but that it is right and proper and quite possible to use either the old or new materials in an entirely new way for up-to-date requirements. So that in chair-making experiments are made with tubular metal and with plywood that are strange to the eye but admirably suited to their purpose.

It may be noticed that constant reference has been made to the well-to-do, to nobles and merchants, to kings and palaces, to castles, manor houses and country houses, but scarcely anything about the poorer people. Until the time of the Civil War between Charles and his Parliament, cottagers and poor folk generally were content with stools or forms. During the reign of Charles II the use of chairs began very slowly to spread, no doubt first in inns for the use of travelling gentlefolk and in the homes of shopkeepers and the like. The makers of chairs for the gentry would no doubt fill in time between orders by making simpler and cheaper chairs for pockets that were not so well lined, or, it may be, for their own homes. The wood-turner had never quite ceased making the Scandinavian type of chair with turned spindles and triangular seat, and had been kept busy with stool and chair legs and arms, etc., from Elizabeth's time. So that so soon as a need arose, first in the inns where men met together, then in the kitchens and servants' quarters of large houses, and lastly in the cottage homes of the people themselves, for cheap " cottage " chairs there arose in well-wooded areas, in Buckinghamshire and in the north, a cheap chair industry. This industry was fostered by a demand for a suitable cheap chair for outdoor use in the tea gardens around London and at fashionable resorts, but more by the effect of the Industrial Revolution in building enormous numbers of workmen's dwellings at the new industrial towns. Each of these tenements required a few " sticks " of furniture, however cheap they might be.

In the south the familiar " Windsor chair " was evolved, the main feature of which was turned spindles for legs, stretchers, backs, etc. They were not the " joined " or " joint " work of

PLATE XXVI

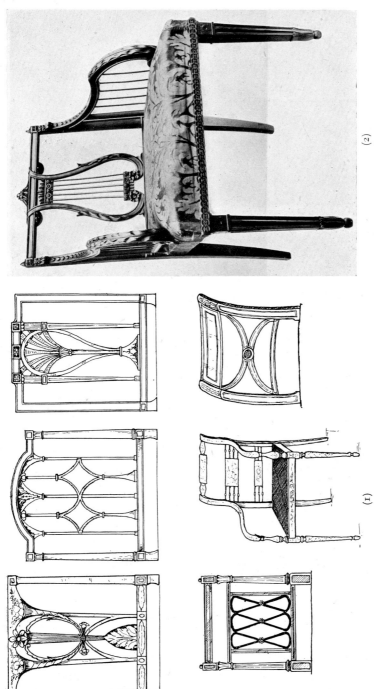

(2)

(1)

SHERATON.—1. Various Backs.   2. Lyre-back Chair (late Eighteenth Century).

PLATE XXVII

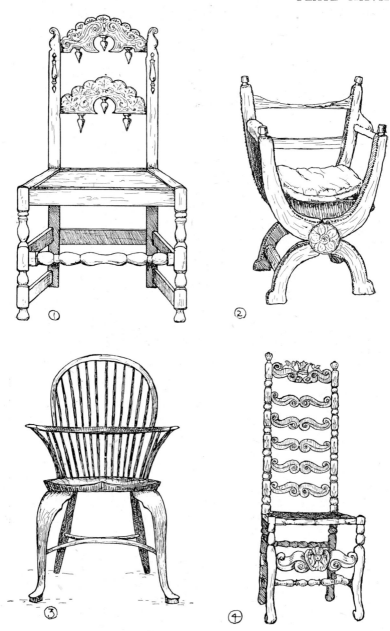

SPECIAL TYPE CHAIRS.—1. Open-back Chair (second half of Seventeenth Century). 2. "X"-shaped Chair, Winchester Cathedral, *circa* 1554. 3. Windsor Chair, *circa* 1710. 4. Ladder-back Chair, *circa* 1660.

cabinet-makers, but were of the kind that carpenters were permitted to make in the old days. They were made of native and not of imported wood, of elm for the seat, yew or ash for the frame, and beech or ash for the spindles. Much of the work, particularly the turning, was done in the woods from which the timber was obtained. An attempt was sometimes made to copy the fashionable modes of the day, and shaped splats were introduced. One design, the " wheelback," became extraordinarily common. At first the Windsor chairs had a top rail at the back, but it was found that if wood were steamed, it could be bent to shape and would retain that shape, and so the " hoop back " was introduced, which was really the precursor of the Austrian " bent-wood " chairs.

In the north, the spindles were sometimes arranged in rows and tiers, and these are called " spindle backs."

The serviceable strength and hard-wearing qualities of the Windsor chair has led to its mode of construction being adopted and adapted for all kinds of purposes, and to-day enormous numbers are produced, not only for house use, but for business premises, schools, halls, churches, institutes, etc.

THINGS TO DO

1. If you are interested in small, delicate craft-work, begin to make a set of models illustrating the historical development of chairs.
2. Include in your sets of drawings, those of chair details : legs, rails and stretchers, whole backs, panels, splats, crestings, arms. Keep these arranged in historical order and *date* where possible (most museums now date as accurately as possible the pieces they show) ; the dated items will help you to date your own undated items.
3. Try to trace the " influences " which determined the construction of the chairs in your own home.
4. Remember that old churches are the happy hunting-ground of students of seats and chairs. *Remember that they are churches* and that it is usually easy to ask permission, especially if you wish to use a camera. If you are drawing detail, a poppy head or a piece of arcading, etc., let your drawing be exact, and put in at least one principal measurement.
5. Begin a *biographical* notebook. If it is loose-leaf, so much the better. You will then be able to build it up in true historical order. Make a note first of all the *persons* mentioned in this book, note their exact dates and the way in which they had to do with furniture.
6. Begin a *tool* notebook. The story of the development of tools will lead you from the stone scraper of the earliest Stone Age to the electrically controlled power presses, etc., of the modern engineering works.

A NOTE ON STOOLS, FORMS AND BENCHES

THE story of these is simple after that of the chair. The essential part of the stool, form, bench or settle is a board or shelf or ledge on which one can sit. The settee and sofa may be regarded as similar, but with upholstered seats, while the couch is lengthened to permit of a reclining position. We have all fairly clear ideas as to their different shapes and purposes :—

The *stool* is a seat for one person. It has no back and is movable.
The *form* is a seat for several persons. It has no back and is movable.
The *bench* is a seat for several persons. It is a fixture and is often placed against a wall which will form a back.
The *settle* is a seat for several persons. It has a high back and may be fixed or movable, and may have ends to give shelter from draughts.

The present-day Swedish word for chair is " stol " (pronounced as " stool "). Originally in England a stool was a seat for one person. " Chair " is French and came in with the Normans, and only the exalted sat upon a chair. It is interesting to note how the names and uses of chair and stool have become so specialised. The stool was the seat of the common person, of the low estate. They are found in offices, in workshops, they were provided for underlings and subordinates, they were put to common uses, there were stools of penitence, and ducking stools, children sat upon stools, and finally they became most lowly, as footstools. A lengthened stool was called a form, a suitable seat for scholars in the mediæval school-hall. In order of progress the boy sat on the first, second, etc., form and so classes are still called forms. In mediæval courts of law every one stood but the Judge, who sat on a raised bench. To-day we speak of a magistrate as being a member of the Bench, and of the Bench of Magistrates, of the King's Bench, etc. The members of the bodies that control the examinations of lawyers (the Inns of Court) are called Benchers. The long seats in Parliament are still called Benches, and Members sit on the Government Benches, or on the Opposition Benches, etc. The Bishops, sitting together in the House of Lords, are called the Bench of Bishops. The old wooden seats in railway carriages, and which are still made for Continental railways, were termed benches.

The simplest stool is the milking stool. This type, with lengthened legs strengthened with turned stretchers, may still be seen in offices, workshops, shops, and as laboratory stools in schools and factories.

The other type of stool did not appear until the carpenter had gained a considerable degree of skill. They are sometimes referred to as fifteenth, or even fourteenth-century stools, but those few we have remaining more likely belong to the sixteenth century. They have solid ends with shaped feet and sides. The ends are tenoned through the seat and are slotted to receive the side rails. The ends were sloped to give a firmer standing and to lessen the risk of straining the pegs that held the stool together. These were of " trestle " construction. The long benches used with the trestle and hall tables were of the same construction. So soon as the joiner had fully mastered the use of the tenon joint, " joint or joyned stools " were made. These were for the use of heavy men in rough times and were correspondingly sturdy in

PLATE XXVIII

STOOLS.—1. Egyptian.   2. Trestle Stool (Mediæval).   3 and 4. Joined Stools,
circa 1600.   5. A " William and Mary " Walnut Stool.   6. Stool with
Carved Stretchers, *circa* 1690.   7. Stool with Cabriole Legs, *circa* 1725.

make. They retained the " box " construction with stout squared rails close to the ground.   They were made of oak and the legs were turned.

Either for sitting purposes or as footstools these have continued to be made down to the present day, following in miniature all the modes and fashions of the chair in decoration and in material.

PLATE XXIX

THE EVOLUTION OF THE TABLE.—1. Finnish Trestle Supports. 2. Trestle at Penshurst. 3. Renaissance Pillar. 4. Pillar with "Bulb." 5 and 6. Supports from a Single Trunk. 7. French Renaissance Table. 8. Table and Form from an Oxford College Hall (Mid-Seventeenth Century).

CHAPTER V

THE TABLE

HERE again we have inherited words from north and south. It would have been better, perhaps, had we kept to the northern name " bord," which is Swedish to-day for " table," and had not adopted the French word " table," for a board is a flat piece of wood, whereas a table may be any flat surface, and a " tab " or " tablet " may be any small flat surface. With regard to the northern derivation, we still speak of a " festive board," while a number of people who gather round a table to do business is called a Board, and the room is a Board Room. Table is used in the same way by Tennyson, who makes the dying King Arthur say, " But now the whole Round Table is dissolved," meaning actually the knights who had gathered around the table. The importance of the table, and of its most important purpose in the service of meals, is shown in its use in " boarding-house " and in the term " bed and board." It is interesting to note the varied uses of " board "—there are notice boards ; chess, dart, draught and backgammon boards ; ironing and drawing boards ; there are blackboards which may not be wood at all. The word " bench," which in woodwork means a stretch of level boards, has come to mean the table-like space upon which a craftsman works, while its French form " banc " has an interesting story. The trestle tables at which money changers sat in market-places were " bancs " and have given the name to the buildings in which money business is transacted, and to the bankers, or people who carry on the business.

Although tables of all kinds must have been well known in Roman Britain, the invading Northmen seem to have made a clean sweep and to have adopted nothing, and the table began once more its development from the very beginning, the board or plank. Some special kinds of table developed from the chest which in its turn again was a child of the plank.

The main purpose of the table to the early Saxons and English was merely a convenience from which to eat. Benches ran around the halls in Saxon and Norman England. When the time came for eating, trestles were placed before the benches and long boards upon the trestles. The boards were narrow and the eaters sat in safety with their backs to the wall while the food was served from the other side. When the meal was over the boards were cleared and table tops and trestles were taken away. Later on the table

40

PLATE XXX

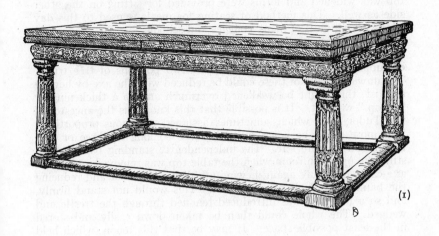

1. DRAW-LEAF TABLE. 2. GATE-LEG TABLE.

top was widened and forms were provided for sitting on the other side as well.   This method of seating for meals is used to this day in the dining halls of many colleges and schools.

The derivation of two forms of trestle can be seen most easily in specimens of peasant craft in Scandinavia.   The simplest method of supporting a plank would be upon two portions of tree trunk. The unwieldy bulk of these could be reduced with the axe by hewing a waist, this might be weakened overmuch and so a thickening or " knop " was left.   It is possible that this knop was the ancestor of the Tudor bulb which sometimes assumed enormous proportions. Still more could be hewn from the base so long as three or four radiating feet were left.   The independently standing baulk would still take up much room when the table top was removed and so the axe came into play again, hewing off all but two feet and reducing the baulk to a thick plank section.   This would not stand firmly, and so a long rail was introduced tenoned through the trestle and wedged.   The whole could then be taken down easily and stored in the least possible space.   It may be that this tenon, which held the construction together so obviously, was the origin of the mortice-and-tenon joint that made all framing possible.   The suitability and convenience of the trestle table was the reason that it was made long after the joiner had the skill to make well-framed tables. These joined tables were made for the use of the " family " and being placed upon the dais were " high tables."   They had not to be taken down or moved after meals, and so were ornately decorated. Some of these tables show the Tudor " bulb " in its extreme form, the leg being almost all bulb.   This exaggerated form, which in some cases was so large that it had to be built up, was toned down by the time of the Stuarts, and the wood-turner was producing stout table legs very similar to those on many a dining table to-day. The carved ornament was greatly simplified until it consisted of little more than simple carving on the frieze.

We have already spoken of the custom arising whereby the family took its meals separately from the servants.   The family would not need so large a table, and yet, when there were guests to be enter-tained, more accommodation would be needed.   This difficulty was got over by means of the " draw-table."   This invention, which probably came from Holland, made it possible by a simple and strong device to double the length of a table at will.   Even in the days of the great furniture-makers of the eighteenth century nothing better was devised, and although the screw extending table of Victoria's days is a rival, the draw-top table still holds its own.

The need for a fairly small table that could be enlarged quickly and simply led to the making of the table with a folding top, or with hinged flaps.   The folding-top table has always been especially devoted to games, chess, dice, backgammon (which was called " tables ") and cards.   The value of a general utility table that took up no great space and yet which could be quickly enlarged led to the very great popularity of the " gate-leg " table.   This made a shy

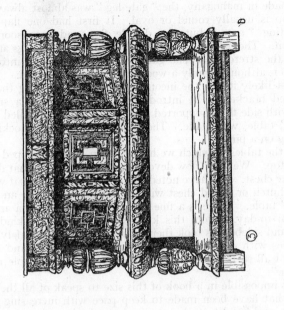

PLATE XXXI

SIDE TABLES.—1. "Chest on Legs." 2. "Octagonal" Table. 3. Elizabethan Court Cupboard.

appearance in Elizabeth's time. Although, in later times, a few were made in mahogany, the " gate-leg " was almost always of oak. The top is usually round or oval. It first had one flap and one supporting " gate," but the double flap and gate soon became common. The only decoration is the turning of the legs and (sometimes) the stretchers. The gate was usually pivoted into rail and stretcher, although rarely a wooden pin hinge was used.

Most likely it was the inconvenience of the gate-leg that caused a hinged bracket to be introduced, and about 1750 a small light table with side flaps supported by wooden brackets ,called a " Pembroke " table, was made. The bracket had an interlocking hinge working on a pin.

All the tables of which we have spoken have developed from the trestle top. We must now devote a moment to those that develpoed from the chest. We have noted that in the Middle Ages it was found that a hutch or raised chest with a table-like lid made an excellent " side " table. There is a fine specimen in the Victoria and Albert Museum to-day. From this kind of table hutch all kinds of side tables and sideboards took their beginning. We can safely say that all tables with drawers and cupboards, pigeon holes and compartments of all sorts have a common ancestor in the simple mediæval " hutch."

It is impossible in a book of this size to speak of all the kinds of tables that have been made to keep pace with increasing needs as comfort and wealth and security have increased. Almost every room in a house has its special kind of table. Bedrooms have dressing tables, studies and libraries have writing tables, there are kitchen tables, hall tables, dining tables, tea tables, occasional tables, coffee tables, there are billiard and card tables, work tables and breakfast tables, all with interesting stories to tell, each with special problems of construction to be solved in order that they should fully satisfy the purpose for which they were made.

THINGS TO DO

1. Devote some pages of your notebook to table legs.
2. If you have a " draw-leaf " or " gate-leg " or " Pembroke " or " extending " table find out " how it works."
3. Make a series of models showing the historic evolution of the table.
4. Make a list of the tables in your own home—with a description of their uses and construction.

PLATE XXXII

(1)

(2)

(3)

SIDE TABLES.—1 and 2. Inlaid Satin-wood, Adam style. 3. Mahogany
Inlaid Sideboard (both Late Eighteenth Century).

PLATE XXXIII

(4)

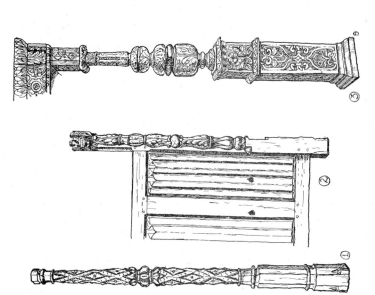

The "Four-poster" Bed.—1 and 3. Corner Posts, (1) Early and (2) Late Sixteenth Century. 2. Part of a Bed-head. 4. Complete Bed.

CHAPTER VI

THE BED

Four corners to my bed,
Four angels at my head,
Matthew, Mark, Luke and John
Bless the bed that I lie on.

As you make your bed, so you must lie in it.—Proverb.

FOR this important piece of furniture we have retained one name only, unchanged from Anglo-Saxon times. It is a contraction of bedstead, "the place of the bed," just as "stead" or "sted" occurs in so many place-names to-day, as in Hampstead, Plumstead, Thaxted, farmstead, homestead, etc. The bed really is the mattress and bed-clothes. It is one of the two necessities of life, which are "bed and board." In olden days it was often regarded as the most valuable piece of furniture.

With regard to the antique world we read, "Their bedsteads were made of wood, which usually came from the Sudan, and consisted of a strong rectangular framework, about 15 to 20 inches high across which was stretched plaited palm fibre, or rope . . . and the pillow was a support made of wood, or ivory, more or less ornamented, with a curved top for the neck to fit into" ("A Guide to the Egyptian Collections in the British Museum"). The hardy Norseman, however, knew little of such a luxury, and slept on straw.

So far as craftsmanship in wood goes, we are not concerned with beds until about 1500. Before that time the very wealthy had "trussing" beds that could be folded (trussed) when they went on their travels. There were "state" beds on which the bedding was supported on a wooden framework. These were so high that a step or long stool was necessary to climb up on to them. The stool was used as a seat by day. There were "trundle" beds that could be trundled under the state bed by day. These were all rare. Poorer people slept on straw or on wooden benches built in recesses, like bunks or berths in ships. There were no separate bedrooms and scarcely any of the privacy we consider to be so necessary to-day.

The draughts of the mediæval dwelling made some form of screen to the bed a necessity. Curtains were suspended from the rafters, or, if the height was too great, from a sort of canopy called a "tester." Tester comes from the Latin "testa," a skull, through a French form

45

meaning a " headpiece," " tête " is French for head. From a tent-like form the tester came to be a rectangular roof slightly larger than the bed. It was in Henry VII's time that the tester was sup-ported by four posts, instead of being hung from the ceiling. Except for the very early beds, " four-poster " is no more than a name, as most of the so-called four-poster beds have but two posts.

The steps followed in the story of the four-poster seem to have been these : (a) the four corner posts of a simple frame were run up to support a cloth tester and curtains ; (b) the bed-head was half-filled with panelling ; (c) the whole of the bed-head was filled with framed panelling. This bed-head supported the tester at one end and did away with the back pair of posts. The tester was made of wood ; (d) the front pair of posts stood independent of the bed-frame, which was called the bed-stock.

These great beds were mainly made when the Renaissance was at its height, and posts, bed-heads and tester were most elaborately carved or inlaid with decoration that copied from Italian work, that, in its turn, was copied from old Roman and Greek work. The two main panels at the bed-head are almost always filled with the round-headed Roman arch. The upper part of the posts is invariably supported by the Tudor bulb, which, in the case of the bed-post seems to have started as a split pomegranate or just a decorated boss, and then to have settled down in the large " chalice and lid " type.

Although these canopied beds continued to be made until 1800, after Elizabeth's reign the woodwork became mainly the framework upon which curtains were draped. These beds were all made for the very well-to-do, and examples have been preserved because of their magnificence, because they were really quite comfortable to use, and in some cases because of sentimental reasons. There were no such reasons for the preservation of the beds of the poorer people and they were removed and destroyed so soon as more suitable and less cumbersome beds could be had. Finally, the iron and brass bedstead came, and only with recent years have furniture-makers begun to give thought again to wooden bed-heads and feet.

CRADLES

Hush-a-by baby, on the tree top,
When the wind blows the cradle will rock.

Having dealt in their turn with the children of the chest and of the table, it would scarcely do to leave this short reference to the bed without a note about the cot and cradle. Cradles are probably as old as any article of furniture, for wherever women worked some convenience to keep the baby from the danger of the ground would be a necessity. Peasant and native craft to-day show many of the cradles of bark and wicker that could be suspended from a bough or a roof rafter when not carried by the mother, and which probably

PLATE XXXIV

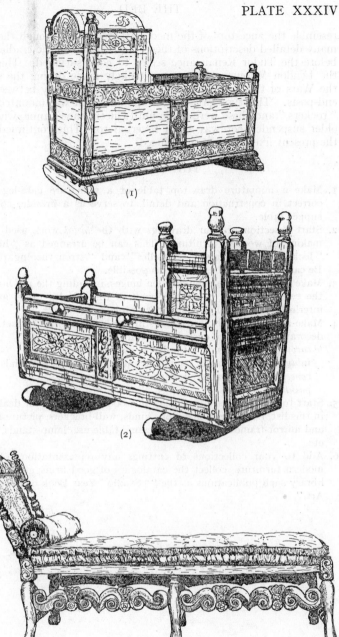

CRADLES AND DAY BED.—1 and 2. Cradles of the Rocker Type (Jacobean).
3. Day Bed of Charles II's Time.

resemble the ancestors of the mediæval cradle. Although there are many detailed descriptions of these, only one authentic cradle made before the Tudor Renaissance seems to have survived. This is in the London Museum and was most likely made during the end of the Wars of the Roses (about 1460). It rocks freely between two end-posts. This type gave way to the kind that was mounted upon "rockers," and these were made until Queen Anne's time, when the older suspended cot was again reverted to. This continued until the present fixed cot was introduced.

THINGS TO DO

1. Make a miniature draw-top table or a miniature gate-leg table, correct in construction and detail, to serve as a fireside, coffee or supper table.
2. Start a section of your drawings with the *metal* work used in the making of wooden furniture. This can be arranged as "hinges," "locks and fastenings," "handles" and "strengthening pieces." Be careful to date these as far as possible.
3. Make a series of specimen wooden hinges, including the pin hinge of the twelfth-century chest, the pivot of the gate-leg table, and the interlocking hinge of the Pembroke table.
4. Make a study of the illustrations in the book, noting the method of decoration applied to each piece of furniture, i.e.
    carving : flat, round, naturalistic, conventional ;
    inlay : string or band, panel, natural, geometrical, materials used ;
    veneer : plain, quartered, parquetry, marquetry ;
    painting.
5. Start to draw, and study articles of wooden furniture not dealt with in this list, i.e. screens of various kinds, wall-brackets, picture-frames and mirror-frames. mirrors for dressing table use, lamp-stands, trays, etc.
6. Add to your collections of cuttings any representations of good modern furniture, collect the catalogues of good firms, get from the library such publications as the " ' Studio ' Year Book of Decorative Art."

NOTES ON THE PLATES

Suggestions as to how to use the illustrations :—

1. The best way to study a thing thoroughly is to draw it exactly. The illustrations have been so chosen and produced that they may serve as copies to be drawn. It is well to draw the article as a whole, giving main care to exact proportion, and then to draw details, each separately.

2. The drawings may serve as the beginning of a collection of drawings of furniture and furniture detail. Draw on separate sheets which can be kept in folders or between stiff boards. If the sheets and folders are punched and tied (shoe laces do excellently) so much the better.

3. Keep your drawings in strict order of subject and arrange the drawings of each subject, so far as may be, in order of development, i.e. according to age. Other sections will soon suggest themselves, i.e. mediaeval decoration, bands of inlay, chair legs, etc.

4. Start collecting. Watch the newspapers and magazines for cuttings, and paste them in your sections.

   Keep an eye on *second-hand furniture shops*, antique shops, and get permission to draw what interests you.

   Visit *museums* of all kinds, but always take pencil and rubber. You will find sheets of white thin cardboard, cut to a convenient shape, and merely held together by a couple of bands of elastic, much easier to manage and better to draw on than the usual drawing or sketch book. You can draw on both sides, and slip each card to the back when finished with.

   Visit all the *churches* you can.

   Get into the habit of measuring where you can.

A cabinet on stand. Compare with the chest on stand of Plate IX. Frontispiece. The cabinet has doors in front of the drawers, but in the same construction. Compare the marquetry design with flowers, birds and butterflies with the clock case of Plate XI, and especially note the " oyster veneer " made of thin slices cut across small stems or branches of the wood.

1. Corner of a wooden coffin. This is perhaps the oldest wooden box Plate I. in the world ; it is at least 6000 years old, and yet the Egyptians were Egyptian able, not only to shape boards, but to use the mortise-and-tenon, Woodcraft. to pierce the width of the boards and to fit dowel rods.

2. Shows the kind of joint used in making the wooden coffins. Some of these were enormous, and very great skill was needed with the bronze tools used in producing perfectly true surfaces.

3. The Egyptian woodworker perfected the method of jointing with the use of pins or dowels. In the case of very thin boards the dowels were often taken further back and so passed across the inside corner. The pegs were sometimes driven through at an angle and the use of the joint (2) checked any tendency to open the joint.

4. Chests, boxes and caskets of this type were common, and show the way in which woodcraft copied from architectural forms. Egyptian woodworkers decorated with inlay, mainly of glass, porcelain, etc., with gilding and covering with thin metal sheets, and with paint. This casket closed by the simple method of inserting the thin end of the lid into a groove and by knotting a thong of leather or cord around the buttons.

5 and 6. Note the support of the reclining back in both, the shaping of the back in 6 (this comfort was not reached in English chairs until the reign of Queen Anne), the animalistic legs, correct for front and rear, which were common in all ages of Egyptian furniture, the " peg-top " or " thimble " feet of the legs, the independence of the legs of 5, and the stretchers of 6.

7. Egyptian chair (now in the British Museum).

You may have seen drawings or photos of far more wonderful examples of the chair-maker's craft in Egypt, but they were the masterpieces of skill made only for the Pharaohs. It would not be true to take them as specimens of what the chair-makers usually made.

Remember that this was made centuries before anyone in Britain started to make stools or chairs at all. It was made with tools of bronze or of hardened copper.

It was made for real hard wear ; the broad seat reminds one of the work of Chippendale in England. Notice the panelled back with the mouldings and the lovely use of simple inlay. Notice the lengthened brackets to the back and the legs to prevent " play." Notice that the workman was sure enough of his construction to leave out any supporting rails to his legs. The wood used by the Egyptian woodworker was brought either from the Sudan down the Nile, or from Syria.

Plate II.

1. Carved bed-post. The Scandinavian people have always been skilled craftsmen. The Danish flint-worker was only equalled and perhaps excelled by the flint-worker of Egypt. Craftwork, both in metal and in wood, was brought to perfection and given a style that is unmistakable. In Norway and Sweden a number of mounds have been excavated and found to contain entire ships with much equipment. The most important of these ship-burial finds was at Oseberg, in Norway. It dated from about the time of King Alfred.

The bed-post shows a full knowledge of the mortise-and-tenon joint. The carving is mainly knife-work. The carved " jacket " around the joint is copied from a leather-work motif. The greater part of the head is the intertwined animal motif which was brought to such perfection later in Irish illuminated manuscript work.

2. The chair is a copy of a very early Norwegian chair now in the University Museum at Oslo. The original is almost as old as the bed-post, and was made in the ninth or tenth century A.D. It was formerly in the church of Tyldalen in the county of Oestadalen (which means the Valley of the East). It is made of pine. The carving again is of the kind that could be done with a knife, and comparing it with the bed-post, it is possible to see that the old

Norwegians were clever at both flat relief and at work in the round. Notice (1) the construction, which is the *box*-construction, (2) the *variety* of the ornament.

1. Egg and tongue, egg and dart, and leaf and dart, and sections of two ovolo mouldings.
2. Various beadings.
3. Palmate bands. Based on plant forms, the lotus, the honeysuckle, etc. This form of running ornament, usually with an alternation of open flower and the bud, are usually in connection with the spiral or tendril, was developed into innumerable forms.
4. The torus or half-round moulding, with the bound bay leaf and the acanthus and star flower.
5. The interlace or plait. The interlacing circle is usually termed the guilloche.
6. (a) The modillion moulding consisting of small rectangular projections probably suggested by exposed beam ends. (b) Nulling moulding which is easily reproduced in woodwork by use of the gouge. (c) An acanthus moulding. The adaptation of the acanthus leaf is perhaps the most common of all Greek ornament forms.
7. (a) Representation in order of a half capital of the Doric, Ionic and Corinthian columns. (b) Roman arch and a roundel or rosette.
8. Greek frets. There is a very great range of these.

Plate III. Greek and Roman Decoration.

Greek and Roman styles of building and of ornamentation had such a very great influence upon furniture, especially that produced from the time of the Renaissance down to the present day, that no time spent in their study is wasted if one wishes to have a real understanding of the furniture.

1. The simplest form. A roughly squared log with a small hollowed-out "money box." The lock has gone.
2. The great dug-out at Wimborne Minster. A larger cavity with a sunken slab lid.
3. An iron-bound dug-out. This has a "coved" lid, that is, with a rounded contour, see 6, 7 and 9. The edges of the lid are iron-bound, and there are two rings for raising the heavy lid. Some examples have the iron-banding extending around the ends as well.
4. The next step by which the great labour of hewing out the log was avoided. It was easier to hew slabs of oak. There was no carpentry or joinery. The slabs were pegged or spiked together and bound more or less thoroughly with iron straps. The projection of the end gave the first foot or stand. In this one the floor slab is tenoned into the end slabs.
5. Another of the several simple constructions by means of which six slabs could be assembled to form a strong chest.
6. A trunk. Showing the origin of the "coved" lid, in this case the upper sawn-off portion of the same log.

6, 7, 8 and 9 show the evolution of the travelling trunk of the Middle Ages and of the trunk of to-day.

Plate IV. Chests: Dug-out and slab constructions.

7. Has the rounded lid formed from a natural log section hollowed out. The end projects, and the under-surface was sometimes grooved to take the rounded end slab of the chest. In many cases the ends and edges of the lid were iron-bound, as they were especially liable to wear and decay. Sometimes the coved lid was " built-up " with narrow longitudinal slabs, either arc-like in con-tour or as in

8. forming the three sides of a hexagon. This one was entirely covered with leather beneath the iron strapping, for better pro-tection against weather, wear and tear, and worms.

9. Although with an original wooden trunk lid, is almost entirely sheathed with iron and is a true strong box. One of the methods by which the trunks were carried by hand or upon the shoulders of a pair or more of men is shown.

10a. The cutting of a small cleft in order that the chest should stand firmly without rocking led to many variations (10b, 11a and b, 12, etc.). Attempts to improve the fastening of the slabs to one another led first to the housing of the front and back pieces, which were usually long, into the end pieces as in

10b and 11a, and also led to the introduction of the BRACKET, as in 12. Sometimes these brackets are incorporated with the frontal slab and form the ancestors to all the later " aprons " of mahogany and walnut bureaux, etc. Grooving starts, as in 10a, where the base slab houses into grooves in the end pieces, while a simple rebate improves upon the previous butt joining.

12. Shows how this simple form of box construction persisted for cen-turies side by side with the most advanced forms of joinery and cabinet-making.

Plate V. 1 and 2. Two poor-boxes. The first is just a tree-trunk on end with a cavity hollowed out and secured with an iron lid. The second is exactly the same in principle, but increasing skill has " turned " the trunk to a shaft and the lidded hole has become a well-" joined " box.

3. Is a thirteenth-century chest decorated with the large " chip-carving " roundels that marked a number of the early chests.

4. Shows the " pin hinge " and slab construction of the thirteenth-century chest. Note how the back stile is slotted to take the rail under the end of the lid, and the pear-shaped iron plate to keep the hinge pin in place. The under edge of the rail here was moulded and tongued and bevelled as in 4a.

4a. Shows the slotted back stile and a very early dovetail groove.

5. The kind of decoration found on the feet of the stiles of some of the thirteenth-century chests.

6. The " incised " arcading of the chest at Hindringham in Norfolk. This is believed to be the only chest with " Norman " (round-headed) arcading.

6a. The incised arcading of the chest at Graveney in Kent. This is one of the very few with " early English " (pointed) arcading.

7. A chest front (in the Saffron Walden Museum) showing a mixture of the roundel and the arcading methods of decoration, probably executed by a country workman in the " chip carving " style.

Three " arcaded " chests. Nos. 1 and 3 show what delightfully **Plate VI.** true renderings careful pencil drawings can give. In many cases the church chests are standing in dark corners or are most difficult to photograph, and then a nice pencil drawing gives much better result. Where the detail is repeated it is only necessary to complete carefully one complete " motif," the rest can be filled in afterwards.

1. Is a thirteenth-century chest at Saltwood in Kent. The tracery is the kind called " geometrical " Early English. Notice how beautifully varied is the tracery at the head of the five " bays," as the main divisions are called, and in the " spandrels " or spaces between the top of the arches. Notice the "trail" or long band at the bottom of two beasts " with " foliated " tails. Notice the carving of the " stiles " or " standards " with wyverns, a kind of dragon with eagle's legs. This is a true church chest with two compartments.

3. Should be studied next. It is one of a group of chests made in Kent. This one is in Faversham Church. It is of thirteenth-century construction, but the arcading goes right across the front face. A " skirting board " is fastened on at the bottom and carved with a " diaper," that is, a geometrical repeat. The carving of No. 1 was all in the solid board, but in the Faversham chest the buttresses are " applied," that is, they are carved separately and then fastened into place.

2. Is a beautiful chest with a very late kind of arcading. Notice that the head of the arches is of the shape called " ogee " and that the tracery is like a network and is called " reticulated " tracery. Compare it with the tracery in the panels of the " Gothic " chair on Plate XVI. The arcading there is quite lost and quite fills the square panels. Note that the carving is now carried to the sides of the chest. The chest is meant to stand flush on the floor and so the skirting board is pierced for ventilation. Notice that the lock is planned as part of the chest and is a beautiful piece of decorative locksmith's work.

There are very few of these late fifteenth-century chests. This one is at Crediton in Devon and there is another at Ipswich. It is probable that they were made in France. This one should be compared carefully with No. 1 on Plate VII.

This plate shows three distinct kinds of chests made abroad.   Plate VII.
1. Is the Dereham chest in East Dereham Church in Norfolk. It was most probably made in Flanders or North Germany, in the late sixteenth or early seventeenth century. It is still arcaded, but the arches lost their points and are the classical rounded again. The buttresses, which were becoming round in No. 2 on Plate VI, have lost their purpose and are just decoration separating the panels. All the delightful floral decoration of the " Gothic " chests has gone.

5

The female figures are carrying the symbols of crafts so that the chest was probably made for some Town Council composed of members of the Guilds working in a town. The centre panel has a very delightful carving of the Nativity below the great lock. Although later in date, this chest is clearly a very near relation to No. 2 on Plate VI.

2. Is an Italian carved chest (Italian chests were called " cassone " singular, " cassoni " plural). Italy did not produce the arcaded chests because her architecture was always classical. She was influenced by her own Roman style and by her nearness to the East. She produced lovely boxes and caskets inlaid with bone and ivory and mother-of-pearl. Her chests, especially the very large bridal chests, were of the finest workmanship. Some were covered with a kind of plaster called gesso which was worked into delicate patterns and then gilded ; others had their whole front panels painted by the best artists, and others, as this example, were most richly carved. The Victoria and Albert Museum at South Kensington has a wonderful collection of cassoni.

3. Is a chest and stand made in cedar-wood in the Tyrol, probably in the late fifteenth or early sixteenth century. The chest is similar in construction to the English thirteenth-century chest, and it lifts clear of the stand which simply raises it from the floor and makes it easy to get at its contents. The decoration is of the kind that is seen in early Italian chests and that became very popular in Switzerland and South Germany. It is the simplest form of flat relief and can be carried out with two tools only—one chisel and a mallet— by any unskilled worker. It is effective if the design gives an even distribution of raised and sunk portions. This chest has a simple geometrical inlay of walnut at the sides.

Plate VIII.   Here are three English chests made after the Renaissance had banished the pointed arch from England and put the rounded arch in its place.

1 and 2 are still arcaded. No. 1 is at Baldock in Herts. Notice that the buttress has disappeared and left a meaningless split pendant in its place. The arches have the S scroll that became very common at the end of the seventeenth century. The frieze has a long " strap and circle " ornament.

2. Is a small chest of the kind called " Nonesuch " chests. They all had representations of the pleasure palace built by Henry VIII at Nonesuch in Surrey. They were all decorated by the kind of inlay called " intarsia " in which the hollows are sunk in the wood to receive the coloured inlay. The Nonesuch chests used a form of inlay that became very common afterwards in cheap boxes. The inlay was made up in geometrical bands and then cut off in lengths as required. If you look carefully you will see how many of these " stock " designs were used in this specimen, and how care was not taken to balance them up. The chest is of oak, the inlay mainly of bog oak (dark) and cherry (light).

NOTES 55

3. Is a delightfully interesting chest (about the time of the end of James I's reign). The arcade has entirely gone and the strongly moulded panel taken its place. The craftsman has become so skilful that he shows off. He raises his panels, he produces round mouldings and octagonal mouldings, his mitreing is perfect and so he makes opportunities of using "broken" mouldings, he forgets that a moulding is just the shaped edge of a panel and makes mouldings separately and "applies" them as separate decoration. The inlay of bone (sometimes ivory) and mother-of-pearl was introduced to England from Spain or Portugal—some say by Philip of Spain when he came to marry Queen Mary. The "bun" feet also came to us from the south.

1. The first stage. Here the upper portion is still a chest, while advance in skill in framing has made it possible to put two convenient drawers at the bottom. The inlay is let into hollows cut into the wood and so is true inlay. Two woods were used, and by cutting the shapes together a variety was possible and this can be traced in almost all the inlay, the light parts in one place becoming dark in another.   Plate IX. Evolution of the Chest of Drawers.

2. Here the drawers have taken the whole of the space, and to save too much bending the chest is raised upon short legs. As the total height is only just over four feet this was a very sensible piece of furniture, but later the pieces were raised to ceiling height as "tall-boys," etc., and in order to reach the top drawers step ladders must have been used. This must have been extremely awkward, and so doors and shelves were substituted iu the upper portion. In decoration the marquetry here has invaded the whole of the panels of the drawer fronts.

This shows purely mahogany furniture at its best. Such pieces were made of mahogany throughout. The workmansbip of construc-tion and fitting was exquisite. The polish has never been surpassed. The delicate precision of the carving appears to be almost too perfect. The wood was faultlessly seasoned and chosen for its purpose.   Plate X. A Bureau.

This piece has "Chippendale" written all over it. Note how architecture still influences woodwork, in the elaborately carved cornice and in the applied quarter columns complete with plinth, base, shaft, and capital. Note in the cornice the use of the Greek acanthus, and the Greek modillion mouldings as well as a characteristic Chippendale fret.

Chippendale himself writes : "Of all the ARTS which are either improved or ornamented by Architecture, that of CABINET-MAKING is . . . capable of receiving as great Assistance from it as any whatever." The column introduced in the bureau is an exact copy of his own drawing of the composite order.

This bureau is really a double chest of drawers, a larger upon a lower. It shows that with all his practical common sense, Chippendale still followed tradition at times, for nothing could be more awkward to reach than the upper drawers.

Plate XI.
Clock Cases.

These long cases have the three parts, the base, the shaft and the hood.
1. The case is decorated with the form of marquetry called arabesque. The whole surface is covered with an intricate but balanced design that was " quartered," that is, used four times around a common centre. Note the square face and the glazed " peep-hole " that were common to the earlier clocks. Note also the two supporting columns of the hood. These are almost always present, but in early examples are often twist turned.
2. Is a lacquered case showing clearly the Chinese influence. This is later than No. 1 and has lost its " peep-hole " but has gained a domed face. A study of these " grandfather " clocks is very helpful, as the clockmakers dated so much of their work, and this helps when considering the cabinet work of the cases.

Plate XII.
Small Boxes.

This plate gives a small selection of boxes. Many, such as tea-caddies, lace and ruffle-boxes, knife-boxes, work-boxes, etc., could not be included for lack of space.
1. Is a casket of carved oak with metal mounts. It is of French make and of the fourteenth century. The drawing only gives the pattern of the front and the centre panel formerly contained the lock. The decoration is purely architectural.
2. Is a reading or writing desk and book-box. It has been restored and has lost its base, but is probably identical with the book-boxes that are mentioned in old manuscripts as standing in the cloisters of the monasteries.
3. Portable writing desks or cabinets were made from the time of the Tudors and were often exquisite little pieces of work. This one is exquisitely decorated within and without in absolute detail, with painted and lacquered representations of flowers and birds. The drawing could not possibly show this and so was left blank.
4. Is a Bible-box. When Bibles were first made available to the people by the printing press, and when it was safe for the laity to possess them, they were for long a very prized possession, and the owners often had special boxes " made to measure " to contain their treasure. A few still contain their original Bible.

Plate XIII.
Hutches and Cupboards.

1. An Alms or Dole Cupboard in St. Alban's Abbey. The Dole Cupboards, which were used for holding the bread which was distributed to the poor in accordance with the terms of charitable bequests, resembled the Livery Cupboards which contained the rations issued to the guests or members of the family in large households. The use of the lathe which came into popular use in the sixteenth century made it possible to produce these cage-like cupboards with their rows of turned spindles, in place of the aumbries and cupboards, etc., with ventilation openings pierced through the solid timber of the panels and doors. Note the alternation of square with turned " bars " ; the architectural nature of the shafts, of the cornice and frieze, etc. ; the square pyramid decoration which is here cut into the solid, but which later was made separately and applied ; and the " cock's-head " hinges which were fastened over the carved decoration of the woodwork.

2. Here the chest is raised upon legs and its top has become fixed so that it becomes a table. Its use as a receptacle is retained by piercing the front and fixing a door, so that the chest becomes a cupboard. The front is pierced so that the cupboard (or aumbry) may contain food. The result may best be described as a sideboard table. It is the ancestor of all sideboards.

3. A standing Livery Cupboard in which ventilation was assured by piercing sides and front panels with a multitude of small holes arranged symmetrically. Had the sloping top been hinged this would have been a " bin." Note variety of decoration : gouge cuts, simple inlay, acanthus lunettes on upper rail, moulding on doors, etc.

4. A chest become a cupboard. Note slab doors and linen-fold panels.

1. The derivation of these two-tiered sideboards from the chest is almost entirely hidden, and survives only in the two narrow drawers in the centre and upper friezes. These were quite small pieces of furniture, this one is only three feet eleven inches high. The decoration is well worth study. There is inlay (of holly and lignum vitæ), egg and tongue on the cornice, flattened classic capitals on the supports ; Renaissance " strap-work " on the cushion frieze ; acanthus, lobing, and " jewel and strap " work on the bulbs, etc. The wood is walnut, which is unusual, and the date the time of James I.

Plate XIV. Sideboard and Court Cupboard.

2. Oak Court Cupboard. These all have the general form for the cupboard space in the base and a recessed cupboard space above, leaving a shelf or standing space in front of it. There is usually a pronounced overhanging frieze with corner supports. These in some cases shrink and become pendants. In some cases the Court Cupboards lengthen to give greater storage space. and in others have a third tier or story. This one has the rather pleasing form of carving whereby the surface is left flat (just outlined where necessary with a veiner) and the background sunk to a shallow depth, giving a very clear relief. This method was used with effect on some of the Italian chests (cassoni) and by later cabinet-makers in England.

1. Bookcase from the Library of Christ Church, Oxford. The keeping of books and manuscripts in chests and cupboards or " presses " was usual as late as the time of the first Stuarts. The earliest bookcases of which we know were ordered by Samuel Pepys. Rich men and learned societies began to gather large collections of bound books and to seek means of storing them so that they should be easily got at. Special rooms were built for them, and as they were a new thing, the architects were given the task of designing the fittings. The architect was trained to think of stone, and so he designed his woodwork as it if were to be of stone. Then the new " libraries " were ordered just when all architects could think of nothing but classical examples. This bookcase is a study in architecture rather than a bookcase.

Plate XV.

2. This is much better as a piece of furniture. It was still designed by the architect, and the top (or pediment) represents an item of Greek temple architecture. The decoration, however, is just

decoration and does not take up room required for the books. The care for the books is shown by the cloth lining to the glass which was to keep the strong light from valuable bindings. This bookcase was made of pine and was painted white with gilt ornament. It is a pity that the whole room cannot be shown, for this is only one of the set of cases designed, and the whole form an excellent example of early room planning in 1765. Even to-day it is not often that room and furniture are planned together.

Plate XVI.   This plate gives two examples of seats with canopies. At first the canopy was definitely a protection against bad weather. Buildings were draughty, especially as most windows were unglazed, and roofs were sometimes leaky. Putting up a canopy was a difficult matter, and so only the seats and beds of the important folk had them, and the canopy came to be regarded as an indication of rank. The monks and other clergy taking part in the lengthy services in ice-cold churches— there were no heating systems—also needed shelter from draughts. So that (1) wealthy people were able to afford skilful workmen to erect and decorate their seats of state, and (2) the protection and sometimes the wealth of the churches attracted skilful workmen who desired to labour in peace. The canopies to the " stalls " and bishops' " thrones " in our churches and cathedrals have some wonderful work.

1. which is the stalls of All Saints, Hereford, is fairly simple work, but if you will look to Plate XVII (No. 4) you will see the detail of the canopy. You will see that, although it is woodwork, it was designed as if it were of stone. Church stalls are no more than separate wall benches such as ran round the halls of manor houses. These clearly show the hinged seats or misericords which here are turned up so that the person could rest on the bracket with arms supported on the side rest.

2. Is a French canopied seat from Tourain. It was most likely a seigniorial chair, that is, the seat only used by the head of a noble family. It was made about 1500. It shows (1) how the chair developed from the chest. If you cover up all the top part you will see exactly how like a chest the seat is. It is still a " locker ". Notice (2) the linen-fold panelling of front and side. Notice (3) how the geometric tracery of the back panels repeats, making a diaper, and compare it with the tracery of the back of the Hereford stalls, and on the middle chest on Plate VI.

Plate XVII.   1, 2 and 3 are the underside of the seats in church stalls which are called
Misericords   misericords. These were carved from blocks of oak and hinged on
and Canopy.   a single stout pin. Plate XVI shows how they rested on a ledge formed by recessing the side support. Nos. 1 and 2 both came from the Church of St. Nicholas in King's Lynn and were probably the work of the same man. He may be the woodcarver portrayed in No. 2. No. 1 shows a man kneeling on a cushion before a prayer desk called a " prie-dieu." These were similar to the Litany desks found in parish churches to-day. There is a service book on the " prie-dieu." The man's hands are together in prayer, and his face is turned up. From his face goes a scroll on which there may have

been painted the first words of his prayer. Behind him is the seat
on which he sat before turning to prayer.

4. There is not room to show a specimen of the wonderful canopy spires
that rose above the stalls and bishops' thrones in church and cathedral.
These three canopies are over stalls in All Saints, Hereford. This is
rather late Gothic work, and the carver was beginning to repeat in
his detail, as is shown in the cresting over the beam. There is still
much strong, clear detail. This work shows clearly crockets, finials,
cusps, pierced tracery, the ogee arch, reticulated or network tracery,
as well as the clever manner in which the arch is brought forward,
something like the prow of a ship, to form the head of the stall.

1. The Dunmow Chair. This is one of the oldest chairs in England **Plate XVIII.**
and was made in the thirteenth century. It has been very badly **Old Chairs.**
damaged. It was probably originally a built-in stall in a church
or abbey, and so was not really a chair at all. The decoration is
purely architectural.

2. Turned, " tourneyed," or thrown chairs were made at various times.
During the reigns of the Tudors they were regarded as valuable
rarities. Those made as this one is were probably exhibitions of
skill on the part of the wood-turner. This skill was turned to good
use during the Commonwealth and later on in chair-making.

3. The Coronation Chair. This is drawn without the supporting lions,
because they are later additions. It is about a century later than
the Dunmow chair. It was made to house the Stone of Destiny that
was brought by Edward the First from Scone in 1296. The stone is
still under the seat. It has been very badly treated.

4. A " Glastonbury " Chair. Collapsible chairs have been made since
the time of the early Egyptians. They were especially valuable in
times when wealthy people journeyed from manor to manor. This
type has always been associated with clerical use and is often to
be found in the chancels of churches. This one dates from about
1550 and a striking feature of the decoration is the Greek guilloche
within the double round-headed arch which was adopted by English
woodworkers after the Renaissance.

1 and 2. Poppy heads exist in such variety that choice was impossible. **Plate XIX.**
In genuine old work no two are alike, although the general form is **Poppy**
usually something like those shown.   **Heads.**

3. The pelican was a very much-favoured bird by the Middle Age
artists and writers, and because of the fable that she pecked her own
breast to nourish her fledglings was taken as representation of the
Church itself. This pelican is crowned. Note how the side of the
stall is recessed so that the seat (misericord) was not only supported but could be raised to an upright position.

4. This hand-hold or grip from a stall in Amiens Cathedral is usually
referred to as the " Hucher," and close to the cathedral is a street
named the " Rue des Huchers." The huchers or huchiers were the
chest-makers and ranked lowest among the woodworkers. Note his
bench stops to keep his board steady while he planes.

Plate XX.
Bench-Ends. Here are four bench-ends, one, the square-cornered one, from Devon. The other three show fine poppy heads. They show how the floor of the pew was raised above the floor of the church. They show different kinds of tracery carving, No. 2 showing the flowing or " flamboyant = flaming " style which was so much used in France, but which in England very quickly gave way to the " perpendicular," which is seen in No. 3. No. 4 is an interesting " transition " design in which the carver mixed the Gothic tracery with Italian Renaissance grotesques and leaf scroll work.

Plate XXI.
Carolean
Chairs. After the severely simple chairs of the Commonwealth time, when the only decoration permitted was turning, the Restoration of the Stuarts in the person of Charles II saw the introduction of very highly decorated furniture. These last three chairs are Restoration chairs.

1. Has two crowns supported by little cupids (or amorini), which were due to the French workmen.
2. Is a child's high chair. Note the peg holes for the foot-rest. It has two forms of turning, the older bobbin turning and the later twist turning. Note how the back is really one panel housed into the two uprights and how both stiles and rails are carved.
3. Is very interesting. Note the crown in the cresting. This was very common indeed in these Restoration chairs. Every one was so very loyal. Note the rose on every part of the frame left square to receive a tenon. Note the Flemish double-C scroll in the back and the Spanish foot. Charles had a Portuguese wife and many Flemish and French workmen came to England to avoid religious persecution.
4. This chair is very similar to the severe " Commonwealth " chairs, although they most often have leather backs and seats. A foot-rest was no longer needed because of dirty floors, and so the front rail is raised out of the way of heals and spurs.

Plate XXII.
Chippendale.
1. Six Chippendale chair backs. There are interlace splats, a Chinese lattice back and a ribbon back.
2. This mahogany chair should be compared with No. 4 on the previous plate. The adaptation of the splat is particularly interesting.

Plate XXIII.
Panel Back
Chairs.
1. Is French and shows the complete box which formed the base of the chair. They all have perfectly straight backs and flat seats.
2. Has the back framed between the two uprights. The box has lost its panels and so shows the skeleton frame. The front legs of this and the other two are partly turned, but are kept square for strength where the tenons enter.
3. Has a crosspiece passing over the top, and this is shaped, or "crested."
4. Has not only this cresting, but has little bracket pieces or " ears " supporting the ends. This represents the finest form of the oak panel-back chair.

Plate XXIV.
William and
Mary, and
Anne.
1. After Charles (and James II) came William of Orange. Chair-makers left the crown out and the little boys and the wild roses. The backs became higher and narrower, and the cresting was placed

on top of the sides instead of between them. The carving became stiff and meaningless and the back panel became narrower until it finally became a single splat.

2. There is much in this walnut chair to show that the makers were increasing in skill. Where were formerly straight lines there are now curves. Note the " cabriole " legs, and the fact that cross rails are dispensed with and only a central stretcher is retained.

3. The central panel here becomes a splat. This chair was lacquered and decorated in the Chinese manner. Note the very great similarity of this chair with the next, a Queen Anne " Hogarth " chair of mahogany.

4. In this chair the makers have at last reached the skill that could do without the rails or stretchers altogether. It is a sort of skeleton chair that was taken by Chippendale and other great makers as the base of their work.

1. Six Hepplewhite chair backs. These show very typical designs. Plate XXV. First is a square back with draped cloth decoration, second a shield Hepplewhite. back with wheat-ear carving, third has the Prince of Wales' feathers, the fourth has the draped cloth, the classical urn and the water-leaf decoration, fifth is the oval back, and the sixth is another shield back with wheat-ears and an interlacing splat.

2. Shows an actual oval back. Note the lines of " husks " at the top of the oval. These are common features of decoration used by the Adam Brothers and were used and copied by fashionable furniture makers of the day.

1. Six Sheraton backs. Sheraton designed a great variety of chairs Plate XXVI. (as well as other furniture). He was a poverty-stricken, professional Sheraton. designer, and so had to follow fashion. Compare No. 1, with its painted, carved and inlaid decoration with the very ugly No. 4. No. 5 is painted, and while one feels it to be very graceful it appears to be very fragile and suited perhaps to a lady's boudoir but not for general use. No. 6 is one belonging to the very brief period of furniture called " Empire," which was inlaid with brass. It was copied from the French furniture made to supply the wants of Napoleon's short time of power.

2. Is the well-known " lyre-back " chair of Sheraton style in the Victoria and Albert Museum. Although the lyre splat and the rods filling the arm panels are freaks there is the square back, the ample seat and the graceful but sturdy legs of Sheraton's good days.

Certain districts have at different times produced furniture quite Plate XXVII different in type and style, or in decoration, to the rest of the country. Odd Chairs. Towards the end of the seventeenth century (i.e. from about 1660) Yorkshire and the North of England produced the kind of chair shown in

1. The box under-framing is retained, the front rail is raised and turned. The seat is really a shallow tray made to hold a flattish " squab " cushion. But the great distinction is that they were the first real open-back chairs.

2. The chair kept in Winchester Cathedral and stated to be that made for the unfortunate Queen Mary and used at her marriage with Philip of Spain (1554). The " X " shaped frame dates from remote antiquity and recurs repeatedly during the Dark and Middle Ages for use by important people. It was, perhaps, the only really comfortable chair of those times. The chair with its padded cushions was probably copied from Italy, and it was not until late in Elizabeth's reign that very wealthy people began to possess such chairs.

3. The wood turner in the south of England (especially in Buckinghamshire) evolved the Windsor chair, the distinguishing feature of which is the " spindle " construction. There are innumerable varieties of Windsor chairs, of which the " wheel back " and the " bent wood " or " bow " back are very well known. Fashionable makers copied the humble Windsor at times and added features such as the cabriole legs here.

4. Another country type of chair which evolved from the high-backed chair of William and Mary is the " ladder back," so named from the number of cross rails in the back. This is a very ornate " Restoration " ladder back. The " rungs " are the Flemish scroll, there are two crowns, one with little supporting " amorini " and the other with the king's head. It has the " Spanish " feet, and two small crowns for finials.

1. An Egyptian hide-seated stool.

2. The kind of stool which is usually referred to as " xiv century " but which more often belong to the next century at least. It is also called the " trestle " stool from its solid ends, which are braced together by the cross-pieces. These stools were either " single " or " long."

3. A " joined " or " joint " stool with a box top. This is really a diminutive chest raised on legs. Note the early " bobbin " turning.

4. A joint stool, later and of lighter construction than No. 3. Compare the inward slope, which gave a stronger seat than the upright, with that of the Egyptian stool.

5. A " walnut stool " of William and Mary's time.

6. A later stool with " serpentine " stretchers and " bun " feet.

7. A " Chippendale " mahogany stool. Note the " claw-and-ball " feet.

1. Two Finnish trestle supports, hewn from the solid trunk. Note the substantial bulb, left to give strength.

2. The trestle at Penshurst. Here the same form as in No. 1 is made by building up round a central baulk.

3. Here is still the same form but with as much as possible trimmed away, leaving the central pillar which is decorated in Renaissance classical style.

4. Here there is still the single column support at the end of the table, but the column is almost swallowed by the great " knop " or " bulb," which is of the " chalice and cover " type. The cover has what is termed " gadroon " ornament, and the chalice has a rather nice acanthus leaf and two little " catherine wheel " inlays. Note the stay or brace to keep the table from sagging.

5. The two sides of a trunk are here hewn away, leaving a very thick baulk. This needs support and so a rail is tenoned and pegged. This type of table could be easily taken down and stored.
6. Has a double rail.
7. A very ornate French Renaissance table end which in its essence is exactly the same as No. 5.
8. The hall table, fixed wall seat and long stools in an Oxford college dining hall. The single pedestal support of the stool repeats the form of 1, 2, 3, etc. Note the sturdy " vase " turning of the legs.

1. A draw table belonging to the beginning of the reign of James I. **Plate XXX.** The legs have lost the bulb and have taken the form of a column **Draw Table** complete with base and shaft and capital. Note the rails of the **and Gate** upper framing. They are " cushion " shaped, carved with a strap- **Leg.** work design and are taken round the upper part of the leg post.
2. There is an enormous variety of gate-leg tables. This one has a double gate. Note the double vase turning.

1. The convenience of the chest for several purposes is mentioned in **Plate XXXI.** the text. This side table is really little more than a chest raised **Side Tables.** on legs. It retains its hinged lid. Note the " lunettes " with the acanthus leaf filling, and also the rosettes in the " spandrels."
2. This side table has several interesting features. First, the awkward arrangement of raising the top is avoided by making the receptacle a " drawer " ; some tables have a cupboard. In small rooms a sharp corner was sometimes an inconvenience, and so here the corners are taken off. This table could be moved from the side to the middle of the room, and the top was doubled and hinged so that it could be rested upon a gate at the back. This method is followed on card tables, etc., to-day. The base is raised from the floor and so forms a kind of shelf.
3. A sideboard or " cupboard buffet." It should be compared with the sideboard ou Plate XIV. These, with the splayed sides, are rare. Note the moulding of the panels, the kind of moulding that became the chief feature of much " Jacobean " furniture. This is a specimen of the most ornate form of the furniture usually referred to as " Elizabethan," although much of it was made in the early years of James I.

1 and 2. The furniture designed by Robert Adam, by Hepplewhite **Plate** and Sheraton and others of their time included very much delicate **XXXII.** and very lovely inlay and veneer. This avoided the fault of the **Side Tables.** most developed form of marquetry, which covered the whole surface with intricate design, by leaving broad surfaces of veneer untouched. This piece was obviously a " show-piece," as any use as a table would hide the beauty of the top. The festoons of " husks " were a favourite device of Adam, while the radiating fan is more usually associated with Sheraton. The fans have sand shading, i.e. the pieces of light-coloured wood were scorched on the edge by holding them in a bath of hot sand.

3. This should be compared with Plates XXXIII, XIV, and the plates of chests. There is here an exquisite perfection of workmanship beyond which one feels it impossible for handcraft to go. The delicacy and fineness of the decoration is contrasted by spaces where the beauty of the natural grain is exposed. Note that there is no attempt to torture the grain into distressing geometrical symmetry by " quartering " or other devices.

Plate XXXIII. The " Four-poster " Bed.

When the " tester " or canopy of the bed ceased to hang from the joists or the rafters and was supported upon uprights there *were four* posts. Later on one end of the tester rested upon the bed-head and there were only *two* posts, those at the foot.

1. One of a set of four posts. This is a transition post. The base is copied from a stone pillar with its stopped chamfers, etc., the shaft has the honey-comb or network design of the early Renaissance, while the split pomegranate which forms the central knop could only have been borrowed from a southern land.

2. Is part of a bed-head in the Victoria and Albert Museum. The post into which the bed-head is framed is crested with an eagle, perhaps the symbol of St. John. The holes were pierced to take the ropes which supported the bed.

3. Is a complete corner post supporting a heavy wooden tester. Although over-decorated with strap-work designs, the acanthus leaf etc., the native craftsman could not forget the English rose. Note how, in the shaft, the pillar and capital seem to strive with the knop and the " chalice " bulb for the mastery.

4. Shows a complete bed. Note (a) the independent foot pillars, (b) the architectural nature of the cornice to the tester, (c) the bed-stead or " stock " which has no foot-board, (d) the bed-head with the characteristic twin arch as its main decoration.

Plate XXXIV. Day Bed and Cradles.

1 and 2. Space will not permit of representation of more than the rocker type of cradle. They all present interesting examples of panelling, and, as they were most usually made for a particular little individual, usually have special care devoted to their design and construction. The numerous hand-holds were to make rocking easy, though the best method was a foot on a rocker end.

The commonest type after the " rocker " was the suspended cot, wherein the cot was hung between uprights at each end. These were made until recent days, when the stationary cot is preferred, although the present " pram " presents all the features of the old cradle.

3. The day bed, which was the forerunner of the couch and the sofa, was the height of pampered luxury attained during the days of the Tudor and Stuart. Queen Elizabeth's day bed is preserved at Penshurst. Most of the few survivors date from the degenerate time of Charles II. This one has all the characteristic features of that time, the crown over the rose, the Flemish scroll, the Spanish foot, the turned-back supports. The back panel could be lowered at convenience and was held by chains around the head of the supports.

INDEX

(*Note.*—The student should supplement this short Index with any word
or term which he has found it necessary to look up.)

PRINTED IN GREAT BRITAIN AT
THE UNIVERSITY PRESS
ABERDEEN